THE UNIVERSE AND OUR PLACE IN IT

STARS AND NEBULAE

Edited by
Nicholas Faulkner and Erik Gregersen

Published in 2019 by Britannica Educational Publishing (a trademark of Encyclopædia Britannica, Inc.) in association with The Rosen Publishing Group, Inc.
29 East 21st Street, New York, NY 10010

Distributed exclusively by Rosen Publishing.
To see additional Britannica Educational Publishing titles, go to rosenpublishing.com.

Britannica Educational Publishing
J.E. Luebering: Executive Director, Core Editorial
Andrea R. Field: Managing Editor, Compton's by Britannica

Rosen Publishing
Nicholas Faulkner: Editor
Brian Garvey: Series Designer / Book Layout
Cindy Reiman: Photography Manager
Sherri Jackson: Photo Researcher

Library of Congress Cataloging-in-Publication Data

Names: Faulkner, Nicholas, editor. | Gregersen, Erik, editor.
Title: Stars and nebulae / edited by Nicholas Faulkner and Erik Gregersen.
Description: New York : Britannica Educational Publishing, in association with Rosen Educational Services, 2019 | Series: The universe and our place in it | Audience: Grades 7–12 | Includes bibliographical references and index.
Identifiers: LCCN 2018007396| ISBN 9781508106029 (library bound) | ISBN 9781508106012 (pbk.)
Subjects: LCSH: Stars—Juvenile literature. | Nebulae—Juvenile literature.
Classification: LCC QB801.7 .S7245 2018 | DDC 523.8—dc23
LC record available at https://lccn.loc.gov/2018007396

Manufactured in the United States of America

Photo credits: Cover (top), p. 1 Carlos Fernandez/Moment/Getty Images; cover (bottom) Outer Space/Shutterstock.com; back cover © iStockphoto.com/lvcandy; pp. 6–7 Hubble SM4 ERO Team—ESA/NASA; pp. 10–11 The Hubble Heritage Team (AURA/STScI/NASA); p. 13 Kean Collection/Getty Images; pp. 17, 25, 29, 33, 47, 49, 65 Encyclopædia Britannica, Inc.; pp. 20, 44 ESA/Hubble/NASA; pp. 31, 98, 100 NASA; pp. 35, 46, 52 Two Micron All Sky Survey (2MASS), a joint project of the University of Massachusetts and the Infrared Processing and Analysis Center/California Institute of Technology, funded by NASA and the National Science Foundation; pp. 38–39 NASA, ESA, H. Bond (STScI), and M. Barstow (University of Leicester); pp. 56–57 Stocktrek Images/Getty Images; p. 68 A. Nota-ESA/NASA; p. 79 © Merriam-Webster Inc.; p. 81 Smithsonian Institution/Science Source; p. 84 NASA/CXC/PSU/G.Pavlov et al.; p. 91 NASA/Science Source; p. 94 NASA, ESA, HEIC, and The Hubble Heritage Team (STScI/AURA); p. 102 Stock Montage/Archive Photos/Getty Images; p. 103 Print Collector/Hulton Archive/Getty Images; p. 105 Paul Fearn/Alamy Stock Photo; interior pages background (blue triangles) DiamondGraphics/Shutterstock.com.

CONTENTS

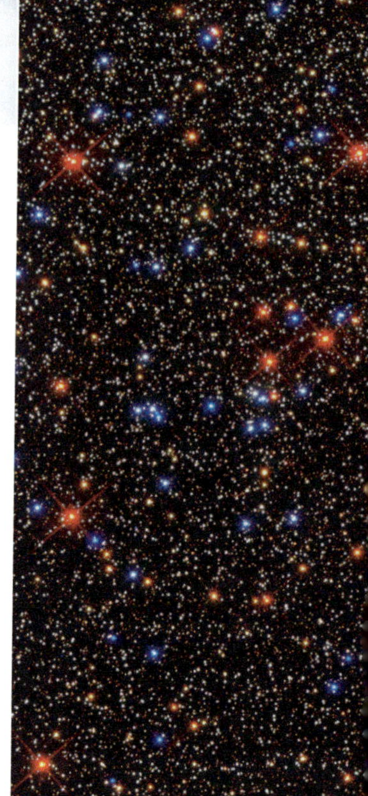

Many ancient cultures believed that the stars were lights attached to a huge dome (the sky) over Earth. The stars maintained fixed positions relative to each other as they moved across the heavens, as if the sky dome were rotating around Earth.

Ancient people imagined patterns in the stars and grouped them into constellations representing various animals, people, mythological heroes, and even everyday objects. Some cultures attributed godlike powers to the stars and worshipped them. Many also thought that the motions of the heavenly bodies corresponded to or foretold events on Earth. This belief, shared by many cultures, became the basis of astrology.

More practically, the motions of the stars (and planets) during the year became the basis for calendars, which were crucial in the development of agriculture. Also, the stars became valuable tools for navigation, especially for seafaring peoples such as the Phoenicians and Pacific Islanders.

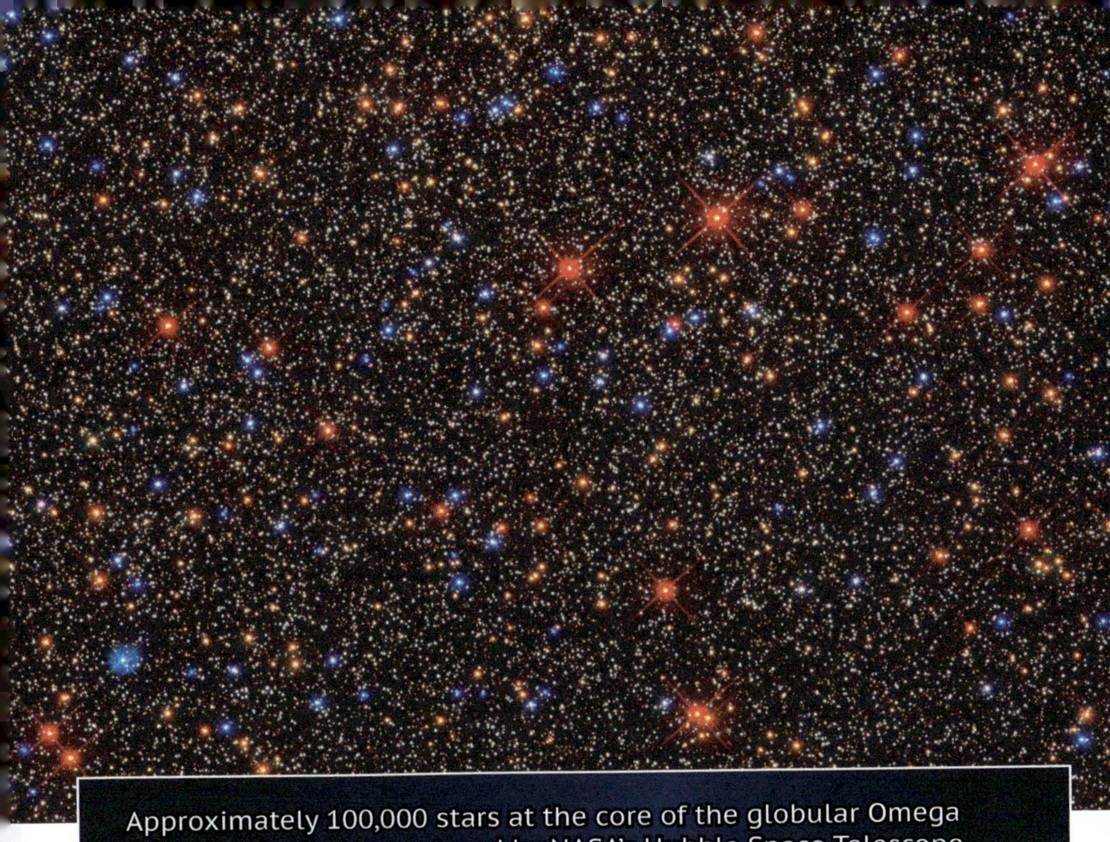

Approximately 100,000 stars at the core of the globular Omega Centauri cluster, as captured by NASA's Hubble Space Telescope.

In the last century, scientists determined what stars are—enormous balls of incandescent gas, powered by nuclear fusion reactions in their cores. However, to just say that stars are balls of gas that shine through the workings of their internal energy does not do justice to their full nature and complexity. Not all stars are like our Sun. Some stars are massive giants doomed to burn away in merely millions of years. Others will have violent and dramatic fates as supernovae, white dwarfs, neutron stars, or even black holes.

When a star "goes supernova," considerable amounts of its matter, equaling the material of several Suns, may be blasted into space with such a burst of energy as to enable the exploding star to outshine its entire home galaxy. Supernovae are characterized by a tremendous, rapid brightening lasting for a few weeks, followed by a slow dimming. A supernova explosion is a cataclysmic event for a star, one that essentially ends its active (i.e., energy-generating) lifetime. Supernovae release many of the heavier elements that make up the components of the solar system, including Earth, into the interstellar medium.

White dwarfs have a mass similar to that of the Sun, but with a radius comparable to that of Earth, making them extremely dense. White dwarfs have average densities approaching 1,000,000 times that of water.

Neutron stars are any of a class of extremely dense, compact stars thought to be composed primarily of neutrons. Their masses range between 1 and 2 times that of the Sun. Having so much mass packed within a ball on the order of 20 km (12 miles) in diameter, a neutron star has a density that can reach that of nuclear values, which is roughly 100 trillion (10^{14}) times the average density of solar matter or of water. This approximates the density inside the atomic nucleus, and in some ways a neutron star can be conceived of as a gigantic nucleus.

A black hole can be formed by the death of a massive star. When such a star has exhausted the internal thermonuclear fuels in its core at the end of its life, the core becomes unstable and gravitationally collapses inward upon itself, and the star's outer layers are blown away. The crushing weight of constituent matter falling in from all sides compresses the dying star to a point of zero volume and infinite density called the singularity, around which nothing, not even light, can escape.

Nebulae are clouds of gas and dust that occur in the space between the stars. A nebula is thus made up of the interstellar medium. Some nebulae give birth to new stars, and dying stars expel nebulae. The Sun was formed roughly 4.5 billion years ago inside a nebula that was produced from a supernova.

For thousands of years, people have gazed at the seemingly infinite number of stars in the night sky. For most of this time, they could only guess about the nature of these pinpoints of light, often making them objects of wonder, worship, comfort, or fear.

THE NATURE OF STARS

In the observable universe, it's estimated that there are roughly as many stars as there are grains of sand on all of the beaches on Earth. There are all different types of stars of all different sizes and ages. Throughout the Milky Way Galaxy (and even near the Sun itself), astronomers have discovered stars that are well evolved or even approaching extinction, or both, as well as occasional stars that must be very young or still in the process of formation. Evolutionary effects on these stars are not negligible, even for a middle-aged star such as the Sun. More massive stars must display more spectacular effects because the rate of conversion of mass into energy is higher. While the Sun produces energy at the rate of about two ergs per gram per second, a more luminous main-sequence star can release energy at a rate some 1,000 times

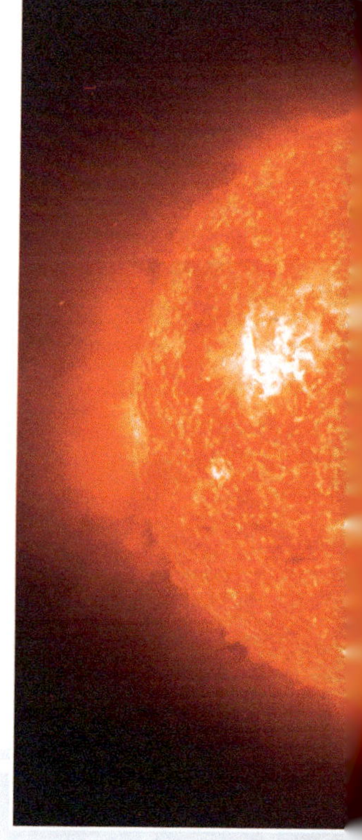

greater. Consequently, effects that require billions of years to be easily recognized in the Sun might occur within a few million years in highly luminous and massive stars. A supergiant star such as Antares, a bright main-sequence star such as Rigel, or even a more modest star such as Sirius cannot have endured as long as the Sun has endured. These stars must have been formed relatively recently.

While roots can be traced back through Arab and Greek contributions, modern astronomy started with the work of Nicolaus Copernicus in Poland in the early 16th century. Copernicus concluded that the Sun, not Earth, was the center of the universe and that Earth was a planet

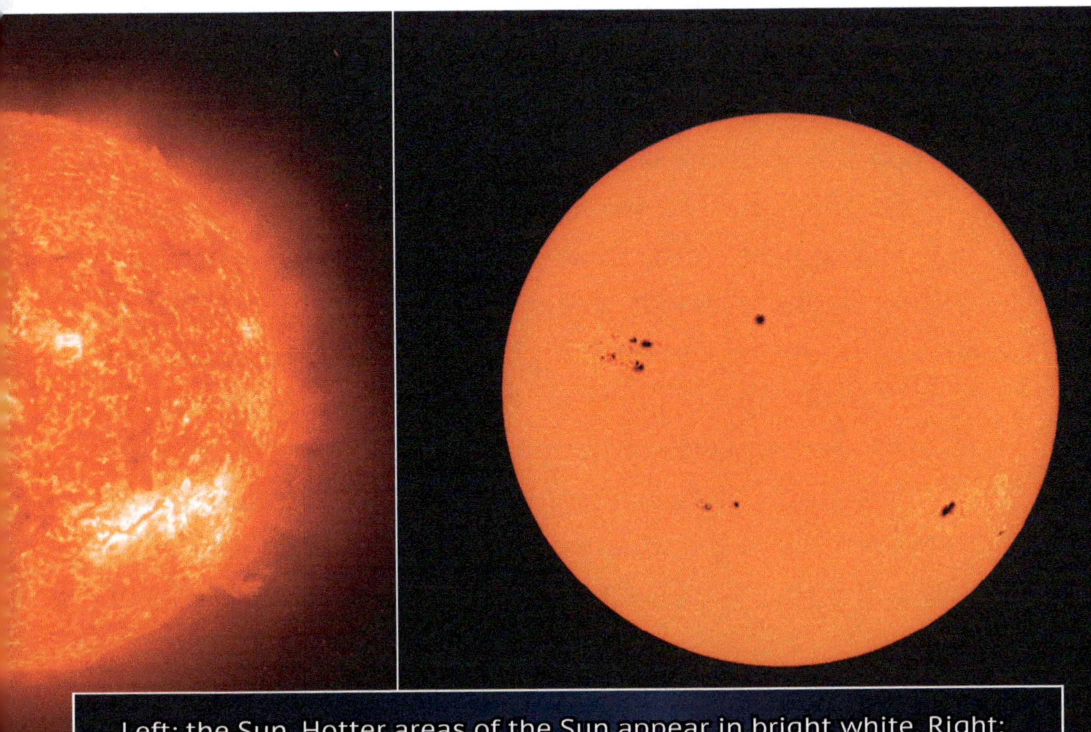

Left: the Sun. Hotter areas of the Sun appear in bright white. Right: limb darkening on the disk of the Sun. Mercury can be seen as a small black dot in the lower middle of the solar disk.

orbiting the Sun. This presented problems, though. One such problem was that if Earth moved, the stars—presumed to be on a large, fixed sphere—should appear to observers on Earth to shift back and forth as Earth orbits the Sun once a year. No such shift, called parallax, was seen. This meant that either Copernicus was wrong or that the stars were so distant (at least hundreds of times more distant than Saturn) that the shift could not be detected. The latter turned out to be the case.

The implication that the stars were so far away led some, such as the Italian scholar Giordano Bruno, to suggest that stars were in fact like the Sun, but so distant that they looked dim. He believed that the stars could even have their own planets. Rather than being on a sphere, they were scattered through infinite space. For this and (mainly) for various theological reasons, the Roman Catholic Church burned Bruno at the stake in 1600.

In 1572 the Danish astronomer Tycho Brahe saw a new star appear in the heavens, only to have it fade away within weeks. Ancient authorities had claimed that the stars were eternal and unchanging. Starting in 1609, Galileo Galilei made observations of the heavens with telescopes. His discoveries generally supported the Copernican theory. Additionally, his telescopes revealed great numbers of stars invisible to the unaided eye. This undermined a popular belief that stars were created solely for the benefit of

Tycho Brahe.

humans. After this, scientists began to think of stars as natural, physical objects, rather than as gods, mystical beings, or portents. Isaac Newton's work in physics in the late 17th century, combined with advances in instrumentation and the study of light, paved the way for great advances in the understanding of stars.

OBSERVING THE MOTIONS OF STARS

Even casual looks at the sky a few hours apart show the stars moving westward during the night. More careful observation shows that they move as if attached to a large sphere surrounding Earth. The sphere's axis of rotation passes through the North and South poles, so that Polaris (the "North Star")—which lies very close to this axis—appears to barely move. This imaginary sphere rotates once every 23 hours and 56 minutes. The 4-minute difference between this rate and the 24-hour day accumulates to 2 hours per month and a whole day in a year. For this reason, the positions of the constellations, as seen at a certain time of night, can be identified with the seasons. For example, Orion culminates (reaches its highest point in the sky) at about midnight in December, but by March it does so at about 6:00 pm. In June this happens at about noon, so that it cannot be seen at night. By September it culminates at about 6:00 am. In December it is back where it started.

An observer at the Equator eventually gets to see all the stars, by waiting all night or all year. An observer at the North Pole sees only the same stars all the time, and these stars appear to go around in horizontal circles. At the South Pole a completely different set of stars is seen. In the midlatitudes there are some stars that never rise, some that never set, and a large number that rise and set daily. Australians get to see Crux (the Southern Cross) but never the Big Dipper. Observers in the northern United States see the Big Dipper but never the Southern Cross. In both countries Orion appears half the time. These motions are due to Earth's daily rotation on its axis, combined with its yearly revolution around the Sun.

Note that the constellations maintain their shapes as the stars appear to move in lock step. The individual stars actually move independently, however. Their very gradual apparent motions will, after hundreds of thousands of years, make the current constellations unrecognizable. Astronomers call these individual apparent motions "proper motion." A star's proper motion, combined with its motion toward or away from the observer, is used to determine the star's actual velocity, relative to the other stars. This speed can be hundreds of miles per second. The distances to stars are so great, however, that these motions are not noticeable to the naked eye over a human lifetime.

MEASURING BRIGHTNESS AND DISTANCE

Stars vary considerably in how bright they appear from Earth. Ancient astronomers devised a rating scale for apparent magnitude, or brightness, that is believed to date back to the Greek astronomer Hipparchus in the 2nd century BCE. In general, the brighter the star, the lower the magnitude. On this simple scale, the brightest stars were ascribed a magnitude of 1, and the dimmest 6. Not all stars given a particular magnitude were of exactly the same brightness, but the scale was useful and has survived (with modifications) to this day.

Modern instruments determine brightness far more precisely. It was found that magnitude 1 stars are roughly 2.5 times as bright as those of magnitude 2; magnitude 2 are about 2.5 times as bright as magnitude 3; and so on. Some stars are dimmer than can be seen with the naked eye and have magnitudes of 7 or more. The faintest stars detected by the largest telescopes are about magnitude 30. Others are brighter than the typical "bright" stars given magnitudes of 1 by Hipparchus, some even having negative magnitudes on this scale. The brightest object in the heavens as seen from Earth—the Sun—has an apparent magnitude of −26.7.

Of course, how bright a star looks depends on its distance from the observer, so distance must be determined in order to learn the true brightness of stars. In Copernicus' time, the annual shift of the apparent positions of the stars could not be seen. Even early telescopes were incapable of detecting it. However, in 1838 Friedrich Wilhelm Bessel used a large telescope to detect the annual parallax of what turned out to be a relatively nearby star: 61 Cygni.

This provided confirmation of Earth's motion around the Sun and also made possible the first calculation of the distance to a star. Using trigonometry and an earlier calculation of the distance to the Sun, Bessel found 61 Cygni to be about 61 trillion miles (98 trillion kilometers) from Earth. A more convenient

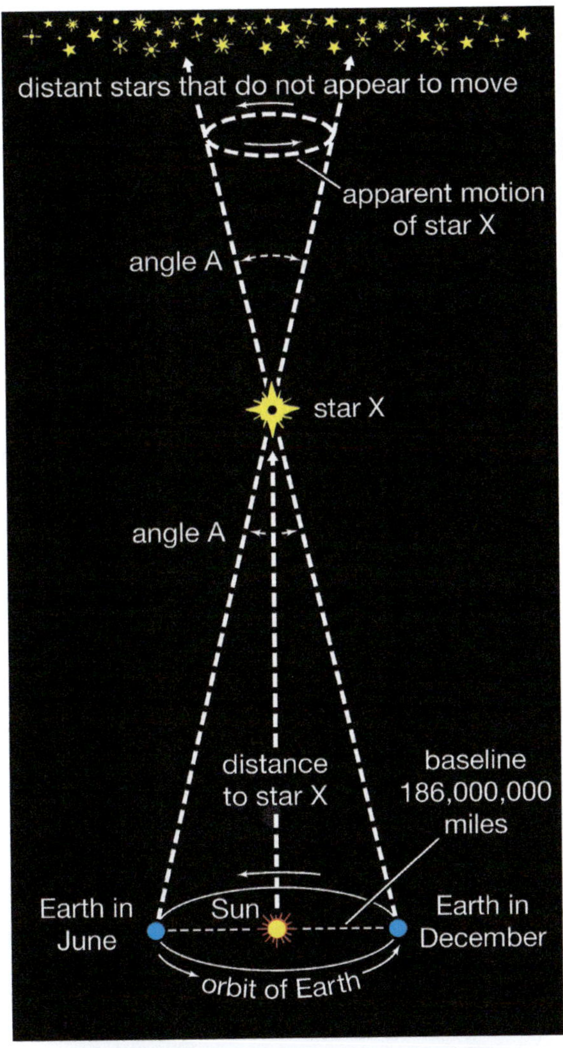

By measuring a star's six-month change in position as shown and the known space across Earth's orbit, the distance to star X can be computed.

unit of distance is the parsec, which is the distance of a star showing a parallax of one arc second (1/3,600 of a degree) when the observer moves one astronomical unit, which is the average distance from Earth to the Sun—about 93 million miles (150 million kilometers). Another unit is the light-year, the distance light travels in one year—about 5.88 trillion miles (9.46 trillion kilometers). One parsec equals about 3.26 light-years. Bessel's distance to 61 Cygni in parsecs was about 3.19, or about 10.4 light-years. (Modern measurements show it slightly farther, at about 11.4 light-years.) The nearest star to Earth other than the Sun is Proxima Centauri, a dim companion of the brighter pair Alpha Centauri A and B. Proxima Centauri is some 1.29 parsecs (4.2 light-years) from Earth.

Once distances to the nearer stars were known, it became possible to compare the actual brightness of stars. One measure of this is absolute magnitude—how bright a star would appear as seen from a distance of 10 parsecs, or 32.6 light-years. Using this scheme, the Sun's −26.7 apparent magnitude would diminish by 31.5 magnitudes if it were moved out to 10 parsecs, rendering an absolute magnitude of 4.8. This means that it would be only dimly visible to the unaided eye. On the other hand, the star Deneb, with an apparent magnitude of about 1.3, would appear 8.4 magnitudes brighter, or about −7.1, if it were brought from its actual distance of about 500 parsecs to only 10 parsecs.

This means that Deneb is actually 60,000 times brighter than the Sun. If it were placed where the Sun is, it would vaporize Earth and the other inner planets.

Luminosity is another measurement used to describe the actual brightness of stars. In astronomy, luminosity is defined as the amount of light an object emits in a given amount of time. Unlike magnitude, luminosity does not depend on the distance between an object and its observer; thus it is an absolute measure of radiant power. Luminosity is usually expressed in terms of solar luminosities. One solar luminosity is equal to the luminosity of the Sun, or 3.85×10^{33} ergs per second. The luminosity of the globular star cluster M13 is equal to 300,000; that is, it is 300,000 times greater than that of the Sun. The most luminous stars emit several million solar luminosities.

COLOUR, TEMPERATURE, AND COMPOSITION

Most people would probably describe stars as "white." However, a careful look shows there are differences. An example is in the familiar constellation Orion, the Hunter. Comparing the star Betelgeuse with the star Rigel shows that Betelgeuse is reddish compared to the slightly bluish Rigel.

In fact, stars generally lie on a spectrum of colour from red, through white, to blue. The physical reason for this is

Stars of varying colour in the globular cluster M12.

well understood: bluer stars are hotter. In fact, the surface temperature of a star can be accurately determined from a careful analysis of the colour. The visible "surface" of Betelgeuse has a temperature of about 3,500 kelvins (K; 5,800 °F), while Rigel is about 11,000 K (19,300 °F). The Sun, which appears almost white, is in between, at 5,800 K (10,000 °F). (The Kelvin temperature scale uses degrees of the same size as Celsius degrees, but it is numbered from absolute zero, −273.15 °C.)

A more careful analysis of a star's light can be made using a spectroscope, which shows just how much light of each wavelength a star gives off. This corresponds to colour—blue has a shorter wavelength than red. Dark "absorption lines" in the spectrum indicate certain wavelengths being absorbed by cooler gases in the star's atmosphere, just above the photosphere, or visible "surface." Comparison to the spectra of chemicals on Earth reveals the composition of the star. It turns out that almost all stars consist primarily of hydrogen, along with a lot of helium. A huge variety of other substances, such as oxygen, carbon, silicon, calcium, iron, and even molecules such as titanium oxide, have been found in stellar spectra as well. Stars are so hot that they consist mostly of plasma, or gas whose electrons have been stripped from the nuclei. Other properties of stars that can be determined using spectroscopes include pressure (which broadens absorption lines), magnetic fields (which split spectral lines in two), and motion toward or away from Earth (which shifts the lines toward the blue or red).

Stars are categorized into spectral types indicated by letters. For historical reasons, the letters are—in order from hottest/bluest to coolest/reddest stars—O, B, A, F, G, K, and M. Numbers 0 through 9 further divide the categories, from hottest to coolest. The Sun, a whitish star, is a type G2.

THE SIZES OF STARS

Stars are so distant that even the most powerful telescopes can actually show (resolve) the disks of only some of the larger, closer stars. For most stars, other methods are required to determine size. One method is to use the Hertzsprung-Russell (H-R) diagram.

A star's position on the H-R diagram gives clues about its size: the upper-right part consists of very large stars, and the lower-left very small. In fact it is possible to accurately estimate a star's size using the diagram. Some red supergiants are more than 100 times the diameter of the Sun and could easily engulf Earth's entire orbit around the Sun. White dwarfs are roughly 1/100 the diameter of the Sun, about the size of Earth itself.

Another way to determine the size of a star is to observe an occultation, such as when the Moon moves in front of a star and rapidly blocks out its light. By timing the dimming of the star as the Moon (or other object) covers it, and knowing the distance to the star, the star's size can be found.

Most stars have companion stars, which they mutually orbit. Often, there are just two, so the system is called a double star or binary star. But other configurations with several individual stars have been found. The multiple nature of some of these star systems is known by direct observation with telescopes. Others are inferred to be multiple through a variety of techniques. The spectrum of what looks like a single star may show mixed stellar types, indicating that multiple stars are present. Alternating blue and red shifts in the spectrum indicate motion toward and away from Earth. This implies that the star is orbiting an unseen other star (or that a large planet is orbiting it). A wavy path of a star against the background of other stars can indicate the same thing. Periodic dips in the brightness of a star can suggest that another star is passing in front of it and then behind it. Detailed studies of such "eclipsing binaries" can yield information about the sizes, brightness, and shapes of both stars.

Regardless of how "a star" is known to be binary, the size of the stars' orbits and their orbital periods (the time it takes to complete one orbit) yield very important information. Using these data and Newton's law of gravitation, the masses of both stars can be calculated. Knowing the mass and the size of a star provides the star's density.

The methods discussed so far have allowed astronomers to determine the size, temperature, composition,

A LOOK AT THE HERTZSPRUNG-RUSSELL (H-R) DIAGRAM

A powerful tool for understanding stars is the H-R diagram, devised independently by Ejnar Hertzsprung and Henry Norris Russell in the 1910s. This diagram plots the absolute magnitude of stars on the vertical axis and the spectral type (effectively measuring colour or temperature) on the horizontal axis. When a large, random selection of stars is plotted, the majority of the dots form a band from upper left (bright and bluish) to lower right (dim and reddish). This is called the main sequence (though it does not indicate progression in time). The Sun is a main-sequence star, more or less in the middle of the chart. Spica is also a main-sequence star, but on the upper-left end of the band. Main-sequence M stars are so dim that telescopes are required to see even the ones closest to Earth.

The H-R diagram provides astronomers with an additional tool, called spectroscopic parallax, for estimating distances to stars too distant for accurate measurement of parallax. A star is judged, for example, to be a main-sequence F7. Comparing its apparent magnitude and estimated (from the diagram) absolute magnitude allows an estimate of its

Hertzsprung-Russell diagram

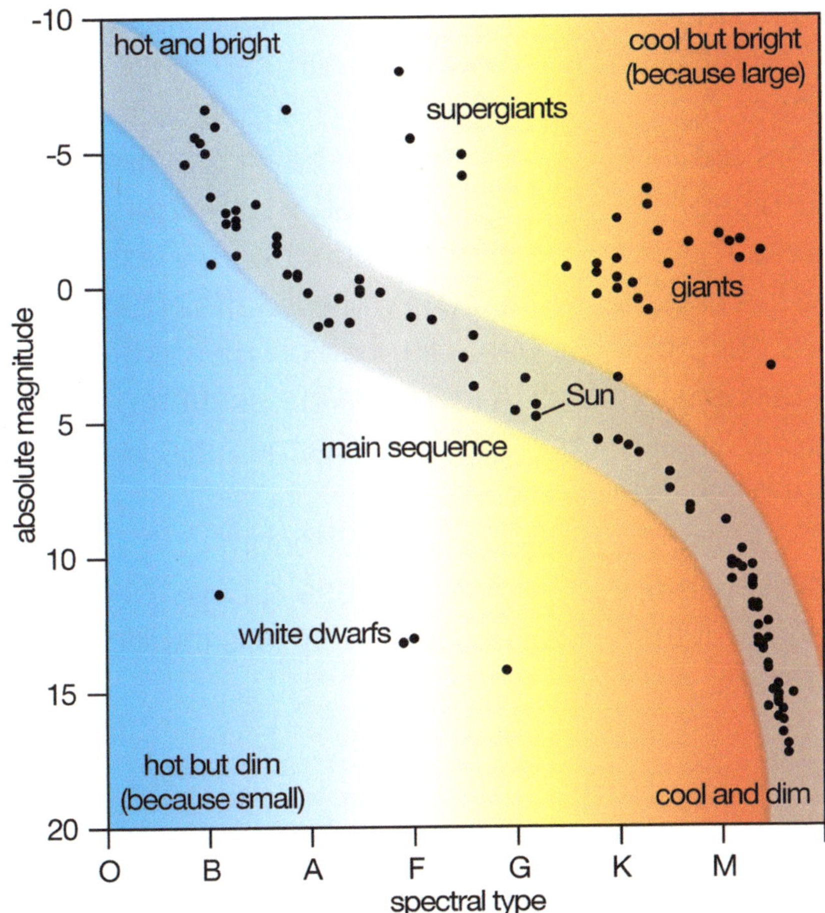

© 2012 Encyclopædia Britannica, Inc.

This Hertzsprung-Russell diagram plots a sampling of the nearest stars and the brightest stars.

(CONTINUED ON THE NEXT PAGE)

(CONTINUED FROM THE PREVIOUS PAGE)

distance. This method can be used even for stars at tremendous distances, in other galaxies.

Not all stars lie on the main sequence. To the upper right are red giants and supergiants. These stars are very bright in spite of having relatively cool surfaces, which do not give off much light per unit area. This means that they must be truly enormous. To the lower left-center are white dwarfs. These stars are quite hot, yet very dim, which means that they must be very small. A few stars are scattered in other areas, such as giant stars above the main sequence but bluer than the red giants.

A great challenge for astronomers has been to explain the existence of these groups of stars. It turns out that the chart effectively tells the life stories of stars.

mass, and density of many stars. This makes it possible to apply the laws of physics to begin to build a mathematical model of stars. What remains is to explain what makes stars shine, to describe how they live and die, and to account for their distribution on the H-R diagram.

HOW STARS SHINE

The first physical explanation offered for the light and heat given off by stars, including the Sun, was that they are simply burning. There are major problems with this explanation, though. First, stars do not contain nearly as much oxygen (needed for burning) as hydrogen. Second, even if they were burning, calculations show that the fuel would be used up quite quickly; the Sun would have burnt out in only a couple thousand years. However, geological evidence and radioactive dating techniques imply that Earth has existed, with the Sun surely shining on it, for more than 4 billion years.

A better explanation was that stars shine by gravitational contraction. Gravity slowly squeezes the star's gases, thus heating them. This can be a significant source of heat for a star just forming but would supply sufficient energy for only a few tens of millions of years.

The current, almost universally accepted explanation involves the nucleus of the atom and the powerful force that holds it together. The vast majority of the energy produced by stars (at least main-sequence ones) comes from nuclear fusion. Through a series of steps that can vary with the mass of the star, low-mass nuclei (mainly hydrogen) are fused together to make higher-mass (mainly helium) nuclei. This generates roughly a million times the energy of burning and much more than gravitational contraction, thus easily explaining how the Sun could shine so brightly for billions of years. Essentially, stars are slow-burning, gigantic hydrogen bombs.

THE MASSES OF STARS

The mass of most stars lies within the range of 0.3 to 3 solar masses. One of the most massive stars determined to date is R136a1, a giant that has perhaps 265 solar masses.

On the low mass side, most stars seem to have at least 0.1 solar mass. The theoretical lower mass limit for an ordinary star is about 0.075 solar mass, for below this value an object cannot attain a central temperature high enough to enable it to shine by nuclear energy. Instead, it may produce a much lower level of energy by gravitational shrinkage. If its mass is not much below the critical 0.075 solar mass value, it will appear as a very cool, dim star known as a brown dwarf. Its evolution is simply to continue cooling toward eventual extinction. At still somewhat lower masses, the object would be a giant planet. Jupiter, with a mass roughly 0.001 that of the Sun, is just such an object, emitting a very low level of energy (apart from reflected sunlight) that is derived from gravitational shrinkage.

Brown dwarfs were late to be discovered, the first unambiguous identification having been made in 1995. It is estimated, however, that hundreds must exist in the solar neighbourhood. An extension of the spectral sequence for objects cooler than M-type stars has been constructed, using L for warmer brown dwarfs and T for cooler ones. A major observational difference between the two types is the absence (in L-type dwarfs) or presence (in T-type dwarfs) of methane in their spectra. The presence of methane in the cooler brown dwarfs emphasizes their similarity to giant planets. Objects even cooler than those of class T have been classified as class Y.

Masses of stars can be found only from binary systems and only if the scale of the orbits of the stars

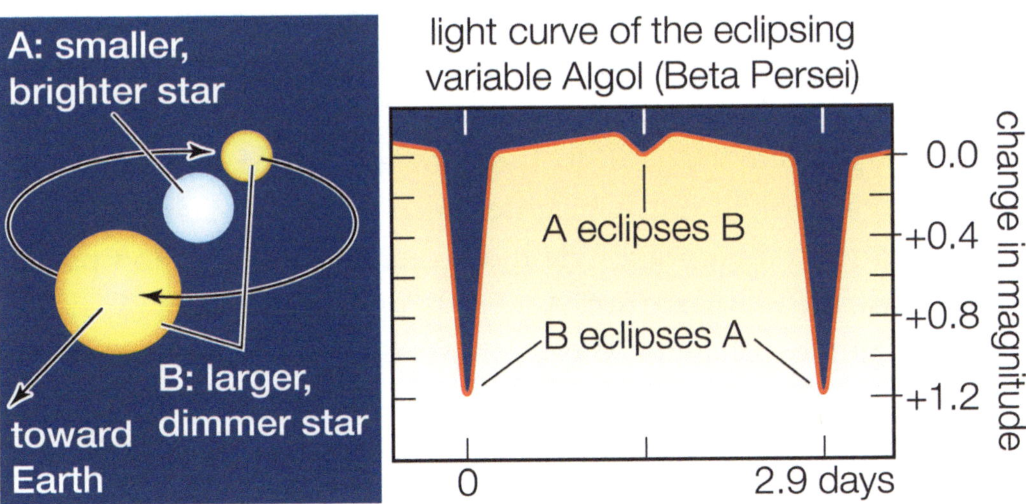

Light curve of Algol (Beta Persei), an eclipsing variable, or eclipsing binary, star system.

around each other is known. Binary stars are divided into three categories, depending on the mode of observation employed: visual binaries, spectroscopic binaries, and eclipsing binaries.

THE VARIETY OF STAR SIZES

With regard to mass, size, and intrinsic brightness, the Sun is a typical star. Its approximate mass is 2×10^{30} kg (about 330,000 Earth masses), its approximate radius 700,000 km (430,000 miles), and its approximate luminosity 4×10^{33} ergs per second (or equivalently 4×10^{23} kilowatts of power). Other stars often have their respective quantities measured in terms of those of the Sun.

Many stars vary in the amount of light they radiate. Stars such as Altair, Alpha Centauri A and B, and Procyon A are called dwarf stars. Their dimensions are roughly comparable to those of the Sun. Sirius A and Vega, though much brighter, also are dwarf stars; their higher temperatures yield a larger rate of emission per unit area. Aldebaran A, Arcturus, and Capella A are examples of giant stars, whose dimensions are much larger than those of the Sun. Observations with an interferometer (an instrument that measures the angle subtended by the diameter of a star at the observer's position), combined with parallax measurements, which yield a star's distance, give sizes of 12 and 22 solar radii for Arcturus and Aldebaran A. Betelgeuse and Antares A are examples of supergiant stars. The latter has a radius some 300 times that of the Sun, whereas the variable star Betelgeuse oscillates between roughly 300 and 600 solar radii.

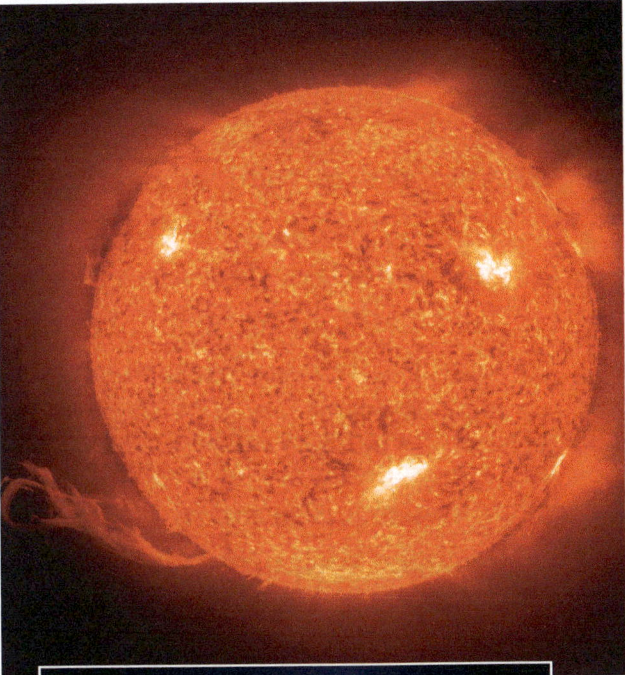

The Sun. A massive loop-shaped eruptive prominence is visible at the lower left. Nearly white areas are the hottest; deeper reds indicate cooler temperatures.

Several of the stellar class of white dwarf stars, which have low luminosities and high densities, also are listed. Sirius B is a prime example, having a radius one-thousandth that of the Sun, which is comparable to the size of Earth. Among other notable stars, Rigel A is a young supergiant in the constellation Orion, and Canopus is a bright beacon in the Southern Hemisphere often used for spacecraft navigation.

STARS LIKE THE SUN

After the method of energy production was identified, astronomers were able to get even more information from their models of stars. Using powerful computers, the physical conditions throughout a star can be simulated. The following "life story" describes the conditions of a star about the mass of the Sun.

Before the star is formed, the matter that will one day compose it is found in a large cloud of gas and dust, called a nebula. Such nebulae are abundant in our galaxy. Mutual gravitation among the particles of the nebula causes it to slowly contract. The contraction may be helped along by shock waves from exploding stars or from other external sources of pressure. Gravitational contraction gradually heats the future star until it begins to shine visibly, appearing much like a mature star. The star is "born" when the temperature at the star's core reaches millions of kelvins—hot enough for the hydrogen nuclei there to move fast enough to collide often enough and hard enough to fuse into helium. The energy released from nuclear fusion produces enough pressure to counteract the inward gravitational pull. The star stabilizes and shines almost steadily for billions of years.

Gradual changes occur, though. As hydrogen in the core is slowly used up and helium "ash" becomes a large

Stellar evolution

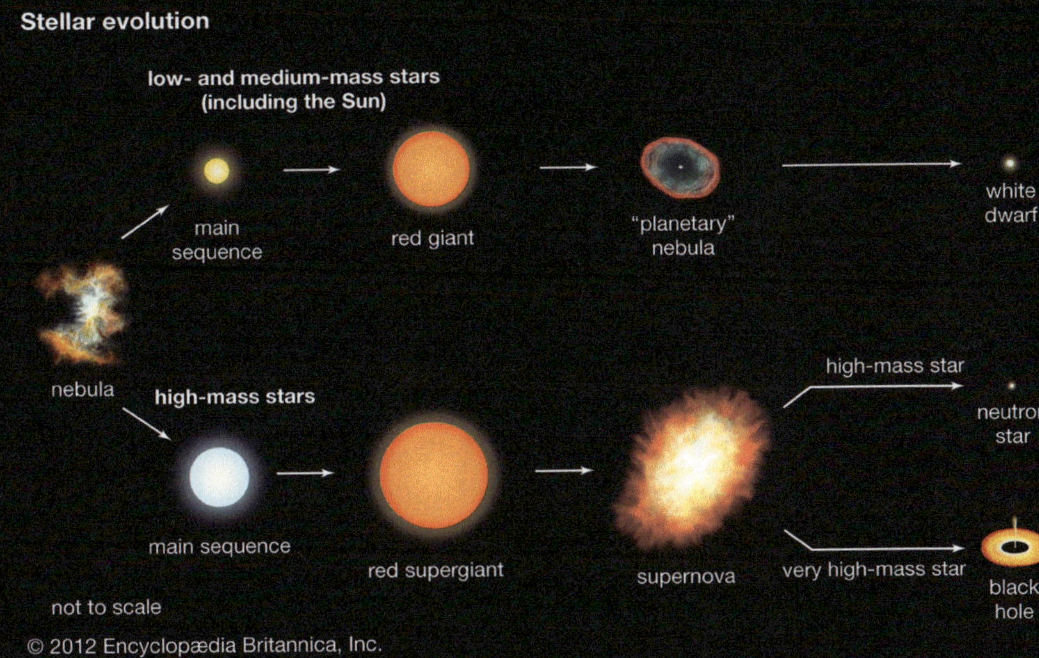

Low- and medium-mass stars ultimately end up as white dwarfs. High-mass stars become neutron stars, while the highest-mass stars end up as black holes.

fraction of the core's composition, models show that the star grows gradually bigger and brighter. After about 5 billion years from its formation (a point the Sun is approaching), the star is about 50 percent brighter and slightly bigger than when it first formed.

This process accelerates over the next few billion years. Eventually, all the hydrogen in the core has been used up. Fusion can no longer take place there but instead starts to occur in a layer surrounding the core. The core itself begins to contract under the force of gravity, thus growing hotter. The star begins to expand, ultimately swelling dramatically into a red giant. On the H-R diagram, the star has spent most of its life in the band of the main sequence, but it now rapidly tracks to the upper right.

The red-giant phase is not stable, though, as core temperatures become high enough for fusion of helium into carbon. This sends the star back in the direction of the main sequence on the diagram. After about 100 million years the helium in the core is used up, though, and the contracting carbon core sends the star back into the red-giant state. The star becomes unstable and begins to pulsate. Finally, in one last spasm, the star ejects almost a third of its mass into space, creating an object known as a "planetary" nebula (it is vaguely similar in appearance to a planet as seen through a telescope). As this cocoon of gases dissipates, it reveals the rapidly shrinking core of what had been a gigantic star.

This shrinking core shines brightly, from leftover heat. With fusion energy no longer available, however, gravity compresses the core to about the size of Earth and to a tremendous density. Further collapse is prevented by electron degeneracy, an effect of quantum mechanics.

The tiny surface area allows heat to escape so slowly that this corpse of a star—called a white dwarf—shines on for billions of years. It cools so gradually that even the first white dwarfs ever formed in the universe are still glowing about the same colour as the Sun.

HOW MANY STARS ARE THERE?

On a clear dark night, far from the artificial lights of a city, one can see as many as 3,000 stars with the unaided eye at a given time. Waiting through the night, as stars rise and set, or through the year, as different stars are visible in different seasons, extends the number of naked-eye stars to about 6,000.

Telescopes reveal millions of stars otherwise too dim to be seen. A hazy band of light—the Milky Way—can often be seen stretching across the sky from dark sites away from city lights. Telescopes show this band to be the combined light of hundreds of millions of stars. Astronomers have determined that we live in this band of stars, which extends to form a huge disk-shaped object called the Milky Way Galaxy. The Sun is but one of more than 100 billion stars in this group.

The Milky Way Galaxy is not the only such group of stars. Billions of

M5 is a large globular cluster in the constellation Serpens.

UNDERSTANDING SPECTRAL ANALYSIS

Spectral analysis is the investigation of stars' characteristics by means of their spectra. The physical processes behind the formation of stellar spectra are well enough understood to permit determinations of temperatures, densities, and chemical compositions of stellar atmospheres. The star studied most extensively is, of course, the Sun, but many others also have been investigated in detail.

The general characteristics of the spectra of stars depend more on temperature variations among the stars than on their chemical differences. Spectral features also depend on the density of the absorbing atmospheric matter, and density in turn is related to a star's surface gravity. Dwarf stars, with great surface gravities, tend to have high atmospheric densities; giants and supergiants, with low surface gravities, have relatively low densities. Hydrogen absorption lines provide a case in point. Normally, an undisturbed atom radiates a very narrow line. If its energy levels are perturbed by charged particles passing nearby, it radiates at a wavelength near its characteristic wavelength. In a hot gas, the range of disturbance of the hydrogen lines is very high, so that the spectral line radiated by the whole mass of gas is spread out considerably; the amount of blurring depends on the density of the gas in a known fashion. Dwarf stars such as Sirius show broad hydrogen features with extensive "wings" where the line fades slowly out into the background, while supergiant stars, with less-dense atmospheres, display relatively narrow hydrogen lines.

galaxies, some containing up to a trillion stars, are scattered across the observable universe, at distances out to at least 12 billion light-years. The number of stars in the observable universe (the universe itself perhaps being infinite) is estimated at roughly 10^{22}—about the number of grains of sand on all the beaches of Earth.

CALCULATING THE DISTANCES OF STARS

Distances to stars were first determined by the technique of trigonometric parallax, a method still used for nearby stars. When the position of a nearby star is measured from two points on opposite sides of Earth's orbit (i.e., six months apart), a small angular (artificial) displacement is observed relative to a background of very remote (essentially fixed) stars. Using the radius of Earth's orbit as the baseline, the distance of the star can be found from the parallactic angle.

Measurements of trigonometric parallaxes are useful for only the nearby stars within a few thousand light-years. In fact, of the billions of stars in the Milky Way Galaxy, only about a billion have had their parallaxes measured with useful accuracy. For more distant stars indirect methods are used. Most of them depend on comparing the intrinsic brightness of a star (found, for example, from its spectrum or other observable property) with its apparent brightness.

OUR NEAREST STARS

Only three stars, Alpha Centauri, Procyon, and Sirius, are among the 20 brightest and the 20 nearest stars. Ironically, most of the relatively nearby stars are dimmer than the Sun and are invisible without the aid of a telescope. By contrast, some of the well-known bright stars outlining the constellations are well beyond several hundred light-years distance from the Sun. The most luminous stars can be seen at great distances, whereas the intrinsically faint stars can be observed only if they are relatively close to Earth.

The brightest and nearest stars fall roughly into three categories: (1) giant stars and

Sirius A and B (*lower left*) photographed by the Hubble Space Telescope.

supergiant stars that are tens or even hundreds of solar radii and extremely low average densities—in fact, several orders of magnitude less than that of water (one gram per cubic centimetre [1 cubic centimetre = .06 cubic inch]); (2) dwarf stars ranging from 0.1 to 5 solar radii and with masses from 0.1 to about 10 solar masses; and (3) white dwarf stars, with masses comparable to that of the Sun but dimensions appropriate to planets, meaning that their average densities are hundreds of thousands of times greater than that of water.

These rough groupings of stars correspond to stages in their life histories. The second category is identified with what is called the main sequence and includes stars that emit energy mainly by converting hydrogen into helium in their cores. The first category comprises stars that have exhausted the hydrogen in their cores and are burning hydrogen within a shell surrounding the core. The white dwarfs represent the final stage in the life of a typical star, when most available sources of energy have been exhausted and the star has become relatively dim.

The large number of binary stars and even multiple systems is notable. These star systems exhibit scales comparable in size to that of the solar system. Some, and perhaps many, of the nearby single stars have invisible (or very dim) companions detectable by their gravitational effects on the primary star; this orbital motion of the unseen member causes the visible star to move toward and away from Earth. Some of the invisible companions have masses roughly that of Earth, which is in the range of planetary rather than stellar dimensions. Current observations suggest that they are genuine planets, though some of the largest companions are merely extremely dim stars (sometimes called brown dwarfs). Nonetheless, a reasonable inference that can be drawn from these data is that double stars and planetary systems are formed by similar evolutionary processes.

THE SUN

Stars vary widely in size, mass, brightness, and longevity. The largest are about 100 times the mass of the Sun and about 10 times the Sun's diameter (while on the main sequence, but later swelling by a factor of 100 as red supergiants). They give off almost a million times as much light as the Sun. These large stars burn their fuel so rapidly that they can exist on the main sequence less than 1/1,000 as long as the Sun. The Sun will remain on the main sequence for an estimated 10 billion years, becoming a white dwarf about a billion years later. The smallest stars, barely able to carry out nuclear fusion in their cores, are roughly 1/10 the Sun's mass, 1/10 its diameter, and 1/1,000 as bright, but they will shine for trillions of years.

The Sun is in some sense an ordinary, midsize, middle-aged star, but its ranking depends on the group of comparison stars. Compared to the stars one sees in the night sky, it is actually quite small and dim. However, one naturally tends to see only the bigger, brighter stars. Comparing the Sun to all the stars (including the ones too dim to see without a telescope), one finds that it is bigger and brighter than about 95 percent of them.

Regardless of how the Sun ranks, its relatively steady, bright light, lasting for billions of years, is ideal for life on Earth. Most stars would not make good substitutes.

CHAPTER 2

UNDERSTANDING STAR CLUSTERS

Though we may imagine stars as solitary bodies in the most remote reaches of space, many can be found in groups, or clusters, that are held together by their mutual gravity. There are two main types of these clusters: open (formerly called galactic) clusters and globular clusters.

Open clusters contain from a dozen to many hundreds of stars, usually in an unsymmetrical arrangement. By contrast, globular clusters are old systems containing thousands to hundreds of thousands of stars closely packed in a symmetrical, roughly spherical form. In addition, groups called associations, made up of a few dozen to hundreds of stars of similar type and common origin whose density in space is less than that of the surrounding field, are also recognized.

Four open clusters have been known from earliest times: the Pleiades and Hyades in the constellation Taurus, Praesepe (the Beehive) in the constellation Cancer, and Coma Berenices. The Pleiades was so important to

M12 is a large globular star cluster in the constellation Ophiuchus.

some early peoples that its rising at sunset determined the start of their year. The appearance of the Coma Berenices cluster to the naked eye led to the naming of its constellation for the hair of Berenice, wife of Ptolemy Euergetes of Egypt (3rd century BCE); it is the only constellation named after a historical figure.

Though several globular clusters, such as Omega Centauri and Messier 13 in the constellation Hercules, are visible to the unaided eye, attention was paid to them only after the invention of the telescope. The first record of a globular cluster, in the constellation Sagittarius, dates to 1665 (it was later named Messier 22); the next, Omega Centauri, was recorded in 1677 by the English astronomer and mathematician Edmond Halley.

Investigations of globular and open clusters greatly aided the understanding of the Milky Way Galaxy. In 1917, from a study of the distances and distributions of globular clusters, the American astronomer Harlow Shapley, then of the Mount Wilson Observatory in California, determined that its galactic centre lies in the Sagittarius region. In 1930, from measurements of angular sizes and distribution of open clusters, Robert J. Trumpler of Lick Observatory in California showed that light is absorbed as it travels through many parts of space.

The discovery of stellar associations depended on knowledge of the characteristics and motions of individual

M21 is a young open star cluster near M20.

stars scattered over a substantial area. In the 1920s it was noticed that young, hot blue stars (spectral types O and B) apparently congregated together. In 1949 Victor A. Ambartsumian, a Soviet astronomer, suggested that these stars are members of physical groupings of stars with a common origin and named them O associations (or OB associations, as they are often designated today). He also applied the term T associations to groups of dwarf, irregular T Tauri variable stars, which were first noted at Mount Wilson Observatory by Alfred Joy.

The study of clusters in external galaxies began in 1847, when Sir John Herschel at the Cape Observatory (in what is now South Africa) published lists of such objects in the nearest galaxies, the Magellanic Clouds. During the 20th century the identification of clusters was extended to more remote galaxies by the use of large reflectors and other more specialized instruments, including Schmidt telescopes.

GLOBULAR CLUSTERS

More than 150 globular clusters were known in the Milky Way Galaxy by the early years of the 21st century. Most are widely scattered in galactic latitude, but about a third of them are concentrated around the galactic centre, as satellite systems in the rich Sagittarius-Scorpius star fields. Individual cluster masses include up to one million suns, and

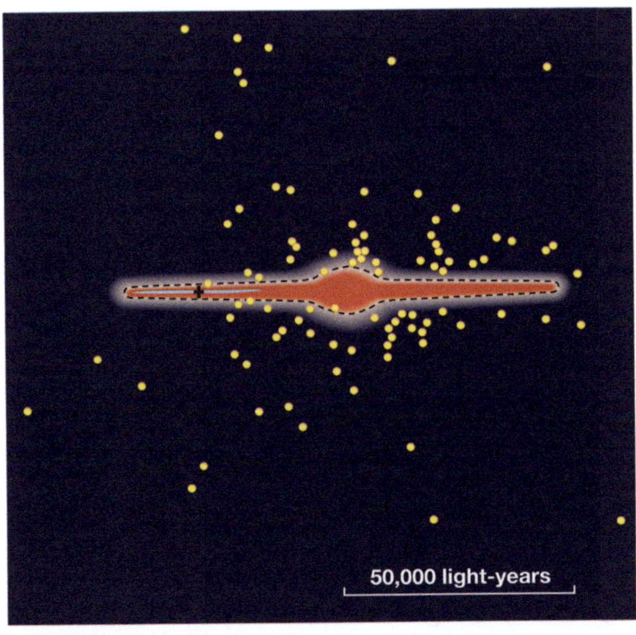

The dotted line indicates the probable outline of the Milky Way Galaxy, a flattened lens-shaped system formed by the stars, as seen edgewise from outside. The eccentric position of the Sun is shown by a cross. Some of the known open clusters are scattered among the stars in the blue-shaded region. Small circles represent globular clusters.

Distribution of open and globular star clusters.

their linear diameters can be several hundred light-years; their apparent diameters range from one degree for Omega Centauri down to knots of one minute of arc. In a cluster such as M3, 90 percent of the light is contained within a diameter of 100 light-years, but star counts and the study of RR Lyrae member stars (whose intrinsic brightness varies regularly within well-known limits) include a larger one of 325 light-years. The clusters differ markedly in the degree to which stars are concentrated at their centres. Most of them appear circular and are probably spherical, but a few (e.g., Omega Centauri) are noticeably elliptical. The most elliptical cluster is M19, its major axis being about double its minor axis.

Globular clusters are composed of Population II objects (i.e., old stars). The brightest stars are the red giants, bright red stars with an absolute magnitude of −2, about 600 times the Sun's brightness or luminosity. In relatively few globular clusters have stars as intrinsically faint as the Sun been measured, and in no such clusters have the faintest stars yet been recorded. The luminosity function for M3 shows that 90 percent of the visual light comes from stars at least twice as bright as the Sun, but more than 90 percent of the cluster mass is made up of fainter stars.

The density near the centres of globular clusters is roughly two stars per cubic light-year, compared with one star per 300 cubic light-years in the solar neighbourhood.

Studies of globular clusters have shown a difference in spectral properties from stars in the solar neighbourhood—a difference that proved to be due to a deficiency of metals in the clusters, which have been classified on the basis of increasing metal abundance.

About 2,000 variable stars are known in the 100 or more globular clusters that have been examined. Of these, perhaps 90 percent are members of the class called RR Lyrae variables. Other variables that occur in globular clusters are Population II Cepheids, RV Tauri, and

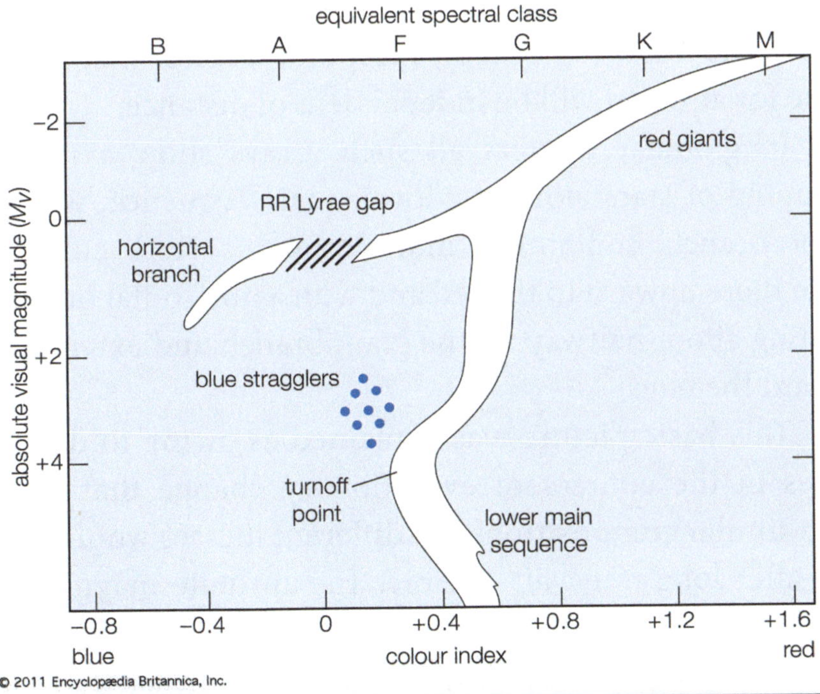

© 2011 Encyclopædia Britannica, Inc.

Colour-magnitude Hertzsprung-Russell diagram for an old globular cluster made up of Population II stars.

U Geminorum stars, as well as Mira stars, eclipsing binaries, and novas.

The colour of a star has been found generally to correspond to its surface temperature, and in a somewhat similar way the type of spectrum shown by a star depends on the degree of excitation of the light-radiating atoms in it and therefore also on the temperature. All stars in a given globular cluster are, within a very small percentage of the total distance, at equal distances from Earth so that the effect of distance on brightness is common to all. Colour-magnitude and spectrum-magnitude diagrams can thus be plotted for the stars of a cluster, and the position of the stars in the array, except for a factor that is the same for all stars, will be independent of distance.

In globular clusters all such arrays show a major grouping of stars along the lower main sequence, with a giant branch containing more-luminous stars curving from there upward to the red and with a horizontal branch starting about halfway up the giant branch and extending toward the blue.

This basic picture was explained as owing to differences in the courses of evolutionary change that stars with similar compositions but different masses would follow after long intervals of time. The absolute magnitude at which the brighter main-sequence stars leave the main sequence (the turnoff point, or "knee") is a measure of the age of the cluster, assuming that most of the stars formed at the same time. Globular clusters in the Milky Way Galaxy prove to be nearly as old as the universe, averaging about 12.5 billion years in age, and ranging between 12.2 billion and 12.8 billion years, although these figures continue to be revised. RR Lyrae variables, when present, lie in a special region of the colour-magnitude diagram called the RR Lyrae gap, near the blue end of the horizontal branch in the diagram.

Two features of globular cluster colour-magnitude diagrams remain enigmatic. The first is the so-called "blue straggler" problem. Blue stragglers are stars located near the lower main sequence, although their temperature and mass indicate that they already should have evolved off the main sequence, like the great majority of other such stars in the cluster. A possible explanation is that a blue straggler is the coalescence of two lower-mass stars in a "born-again" scenario that turned them into a single, more-massive, and seemingly younger star farther up the main sequence, although this does not fit all cases.

The other enigma is referred to as the "second parameter" problem. Apart from the obvious effect of age, the shape and extent of the various sequences in a globular cluster's colour-magnitude diagram are governed by the abundance of metals in the chemical makeup of the cluster's members. This is the "first parameter." Nevertheless, there

M2 is one of the brightest globular clusters in the sky.

are cases in which two clusters, seemingly almost identical in age and metal abundance, show horizontal branches that are quite different: one may be short and stubby, and the other may extend far toward the blue. There is thus evidently another, as-yet-unidentified parameter involved. Stellar rotation has been mooted as a possible second parameter, but that now seems unlikely.

Integrated magnitudes (measurements of the total brightness of the cluster), cluster diameters, and the mean magnitude of the 25 brightest stars made possible the first distance determinations on the basis of the assumption that the apparent differences were due entirely to distance. However, the two best methods of determining a globular cluster's distance are comparing the location of the main sequence on the colour-magnitude diagram with that of stars close to the globular cluster in the sky and using the apparent magnitudes of the globular cluster's RR Lyrae variables. The correction factor for interstellar reddening, which is caused by the presence of intervening matter that absorbs and reddens stellar light, is substantial for many globular clusters but small for those in high galactic latitudes, away from the plane of the Milky Way. Distances range from about 7,200 light-years for M4 to an intergalactic distance of 400,000 light-years for the cluster called AM-1.

The radial velocities (the speeds at which objects approach or recede from an observer, taken as positive when the distance is increasing) measured by the Doppler effect have been determined from integrated spectra for more than 140 globular clusters. The largest negative velocity is 411 km/sec (kilometres per second) for NGC 6934, while the largest positive velocity is 494 km/sec for NGC 3201. These velocities suggest that the globular clusters are moving around the galactic centre in highly elliptical orbits. The globular cluster system as a whole has a rotational velocity of about 180 km/sec relative to the Sun, or 30 km/sec on an absolute basis. For some clusters, motions of the individual stars around the massive centre have actually been observed and measured. Though proper motions of the clusters are very small, those for individual stars provide a useful criterion for cluster membership.

The two globular clusters of highest absolute luminosity are in the Southern Hemisphere in the constellations

Centaurus and Tucana. Omega Centauri, with an (integrated) absolute visual magnitude of −10.26, is the richest cluster in variables, with nearly 200 known in the early 21st century. From this large group, three types of RR Lyrae stars were first distinguished in 1902. Omega Centauri is relatively nearby, at a distance of 17,000 light-years, and it lacks a sharp nucleus.

The cluster designated 47 Tucanae (NGC 104), with an absolute visual magnitude of −9.42 at a similar distance of 14,700 light-years, has a different appearance with strong central concentration. It is located near the Small Magellanic Cloud but is not connected with it. For an observer situated at the centre of this great cluster, the sky would have the brightness of twilight on Earth because of the light of the thousands of stars nearby.

In the Northern Hemisphere, M13 in the constellation Hercules is the easiest to see and is the best known. At a distance of 23,000 light-years, it has been thoroughly investigated and is relatively poor in variables. M3 in Canes Venatici, 33,000 light-years away, is the cluster second richest in variables, with well more than 200 known. Investigation of these variables resulted in the placement of the RR Lyrae stars in a special region of the colour-magnitude diagram.

OPEN CLUSTERS

Open clusters are strongly concentrated toward the Milky Way. They form a flattened disklike system 2,000 light-years thick, with a diameter of about 30,000 light-years. The younger clusters serve to trace the spiral arms of the Galaxy, since they are found invariably to lie in them. Very distant clusters are hard to detect against the rich Milky Way background. A classification based on central concentration and richness is used and has been extended to nearly 1,000 open clusters. Probably about half the known open clusters contain fewer than 100 stars, but the richest have 1,000 or more.

The linear diameters range from the largest, 75 light-years, down to 5 light-years. Increasingly, it has been found that a large halo of actual cluster members surrounds the more-noticeable core and extends the diameter severalfold. Cluster membership is established through common motion, common distances, and so on. Tidal forces and stellar encounters lead to the disintegration of open clusters over long periods of time as stars "evaporate" from the cluster.

Stars of all spectral classes from O to M (high to low temperatures) are found in open clusters, but the frequency of types varies from one cluster to another, as does concentration near the centre. In some (O or OB clusters),

NGC 6705, know as the Wild Duck Cluster, is a rich open cluster located over 6,000 light-years from Earth.

the brightest stars are blue, very hot spectral types O or B. In others, they are whitish yellow, cooler spectral type F. High-luminosity stars are more common than in the solar neighbourhood, and dwarfs are much more scarce. The brightest stars in some open clusters are 150,000 times as bright as the Sun. The luminosity of the brightest stars at the upper end of the main sequence varies in clusters from

about −8 to −2 visual magnitude. (Visual magnitude is a magnitude measured through a yellow filter, the term arising because the eye is most sensitive to yellow light.)

Because of the high luminosity of their brightest stars, some open clusters have a total luminosity as bright as that of some globular clusters (absolute magnitude of −8), which contain thousands of times as many stars. In the centre of rich clusters, the stars may be only one light-year apart. The density can be 100 times that of the solar neighbourhood. In some, such as the Pleiades and the Orion clusters, nebulosity is a prominent feature, while others have none. In clusters younger than 25 million years, masses of neutral hydrogen extending over three times the optical diameter of the cluster have been detected with radio telescopes. Many of the OB clusters mentioned above contain globules—relatively small, apparently spherical regions of absorbing matter. The most-numerous variables connected with young open clusters are the T Tauri type and related stars that occur by the hundreds in some nebulous regions of the sky. Conspicuously absent from open clusters is the type most common in globular clusters, the RR Lyrae stars. Other variables include eclipsing binary stars (both Algol type and contact

OB AND T ASSOCIATIONS

The chief distinguishing feature of the members of a stellar association is that the large majority of constituent stars have similar physical characteristics. An OB association consists of many hot blue-giant stars, spectral classes O and B, and a relatively small number of other objects. A T association consists of cooler dwarf stars, many of which exhibit irregular variations in brightness. The stars clearly must be relatively close to each other in space, though in some cases they might be widely dispersed in the sky and are less closely placed than in the open clusters.

The existence of an OB association is usually established through a study of the space distribution of early O- and B-type stars. It appears as a concentration of points in a three-dimensional plot of galactic longitude and latitude and distance. More than 70 have been cataloged and are designated by constellation abbreviation and number (e.g., Per OB 1 in the constellation Perseus). In terms of dimensions, they are larger than open clusters, ranging from 100 to 700 light-years in diameter, and usually contain one or more open clusters as nuclei. They frequently contain a special type of multiple star, the Trapezium (named for its prototype in Orion), as well as supergiants, binaries, gaseous nebulas, and globules. Associations are relatively homogeneous in age. The best distance determinations are from spectroscopic parallaxes of individual stars—i.e., estimates of their absolute magnitudes made from studies of their spectra. Most of those known are closer than 10,000 light-years, with the nearest association, straddling the boundary between Centaurus and Crux, at 385 light-years.

Associations appear to be almost spherical, though rapid elongation would be expected from the shearing effect of differential galactic rotation. Expansion, which is on the order of 10 km/sec, may well mask the tendency to elongate, and this is confirmed in some. Tidal forces break up an association in less than 10 million years through differences in the attraction by an outside body on members in different parts of the association.

A good example of an OB association is Per OB 1, at a distance of some 7,500 light-years. A large group of 20 supergiant stars of spectral type M belongs to Per OB 1. Associations with red supergiants may be in a relatively advanced evolutionary stage, almost ready to disintegrate.

The T associations (short for T Tauri associations) are formed by groups of T Tauri stars associated with

(CONTINUED ON THE NEXT PAGE)

(CONTINUED FROM THE PREVIOUS PAGE)

the clouds of interstellar matter (nebulas) in which they occur. About three dozen are recognized. A T Tauri star is characterized by irregular variations of light, low luminosity, and hydrogen line (H-alpha) emission. It is a newly formed star of intermediate mass that is still in the process of contraction from diffuse matter. The small motions of T Tauri stars relative to a given nebula indicate that they are not field stars passing through the nebula. They are found in greatest numbers in regions with bright O- and B-type stars.

T associations occur only in or near regions of galactic nebulosity, either bright or dark, and only in obscured regions showing the presence of dust. Besides T Tauri stars, they include related variables, nonvariable stars, and Herbig-Haro objects—small nebulosities 10,000 astronomical units in diameter, each containing several starlike condensations in configurations similar to the Trapezium, Theta Orionis, in the sword of Orion. These objects are considered to be star groups at the very beginning of life.

The constellation of Cygnus has five T associations, and Orion and Taurus have four each. The richest is Ori T2, with more than 400 members; it has a diameter of 50 by 90 light-years and lies at a distance of 1,300 light-years around the variable star T Ori.

binaries), flare stars, and spectrum variables, such as Pleione. The last-named star, one of the Pleiades, is known to cast off shells of matter from time to time, perhaps as a result of its high rotational speed (up to 322 km/sec). About two dozen open clusters are known to contain Population I Cepheids, and since the distances of these clusters can be determined accurately, the absolute magnitudes of those Cepheids are well determined. This has been of paramount importance in calibrating the period-luminosity relation for Cepheids, and thus in determining the distance scale of the universe.

The colour- or spectrum-magnitude diagram derived from the individual stars holds vital information. Colour-magnitude diagrams are available for about 200 clusters on the UBV photometric system, in which colour is measured from the amount of light radiated by the stars in the ultraviolet, blue, and visual (yellow) wavelength regions. In young clusters, stars are found along the luminous bright blue branch, whereas in old clusters, beyond a turnoff only a magnitude or two brighter than the Sun, they are red giants and supergiants.

Distances can be determined by many methods—geometric, photometric, and spectroscopic—with corrections for interstellar absorption. For the very nearest clusters, direct (trigonometric) parallaxes may be obtained, and these are inversely proportional to the distance. Distances can be derived from proper motions, apparent magnitudes of the brightest stars, and spectroscopically from individual bright stars. Colour-magnitude diagrams, fitted to a standard plot of the main sequence, provide a common and reliable tool for determining distance. The nearest open cluster is the nucleus of the Ursa Major group at a distance of 65 light-years; the farthest clusters are thousands of light-years away.

Motions, including radial velocities and proper motion, have been measured for thousands of cluster stars. The radial velocities of open cluster stars are much smaller than those of globular clusters, averaging tens of kilometres per second, but their proper motions are larger. Open clusters share in the galactic rotation. Used with galactic-rotation formulas, the radial velocities provide another means of distance determination.

A few clusters are known as moving clusters because the convergence of the proper motions of their individual stars toward a "convergent point" is pronounced. The apparent convergence is caused by perspective: the cluster members are really moving as a swarm in almost parallel directions and with about the same speeds. The Hyades is the most-prominent example of a moving cluster. (The Hyades stars are converging with a velocity of 45 km/sec toward the point in the sky with position coordinates right ascension 94 arc degrees, declination +7.6 arc degrees.)

The Ursa Major group, another moving cluster, occupies a volume of space containing the Sun, but the Sun is not a member. The cluster consists of a compact nucleus of 14 stars and an extended stream.

Stellar groups are composed of stars presumed to have been formed together in a batch, but the members are now too widely separated to be recognized as a cluster.

Of all the open clusters, the Pleiades is the best known and perhaps the most thoroughly studied. This cluster, with a diameter of 35 light-years at a distance of 440 light-years, is composed of about 1,000 stars and is 100 million years old. Near the Pleiades in the sky but not so conspicuous, the Hyades is the second nearest cluster at 150 light-years. Its stars are similar to those in the solar neighbourhood, and it is an older cluster (about 615 million years in age). Measurements of the Hyades long formed a basis for astronomical determinations of distance and age because its thoroughly studied main sequence was used as a standard. The higher-than-usual metal abundance in its stars, however, complicated matters, and it is no longer favoured in this way. Coma Berenices, located 290 light-years away, is an example of a "poor" cluster, containing only about 40 stars. There are some extremely young open clusters. Of these, the one associated with the Orion Nebula, which is some 4 million years old, is the closest, at a distance of 1,400 light-years. A still younger cluster is NGC 6611, some of the stars in which formed only a few hundred thousand years ago. At the other end of the scale, some open clusters have ages approaching those of the globular clusters. M67 in the constellation Cancer is 4.5 billion years old, and NGC 188 in Cepheus is 6.5 billion years of age. The oldest known open cluster, Collinder 261 in the southern constellation of Musca, is 8.9 billion years old.

THE NATURE OF STAR CLUSTERS

Seen from intergalactic space, the Milky Way Galaxy would appear as a giant luminous pinwheel, with more than 150 globular clusters dotted around it. The richest parts of the spiral arms of the pinwheel would be marked by dozens of open clusters. If this panorama could be seen as a time-lapse movie, the great globular clusters would wheel around the galactic centre in elliptical orbits with periods of hundreds of millions of years. The open clusters and stellar associations would be seen to form out of knots of diffuse matter in the spiral arms, gradually disperse, run through their life cycle, and fade away, while the Sun pursued its course around the galactic centre for billions of years.

Young open clusters and associations, occupying the same region of space as clouds of ionized hydrogen (gaseous nebulas), help to define the spiral arms. A concentration of clusters in the bright inner portion of the Milky

Way between galactic longitudes 283° and 28° indicates an inner arm in Sagittarius. Similarly, the two spiral arms of Orion and Perseus are defined between 103° and 213°, with a bifurcation of the Orion arm. Associations show the existence of spiral structure in the Sun's vicinity. Older clusters, whose main sequence does not reach to the blue stars, show no correlation with spiral arms because in the intervening years their motions have carried them far from their place of birth.

All the O- and B-type stars in the Galaxy might have originated in OB associations. The great majority, if not

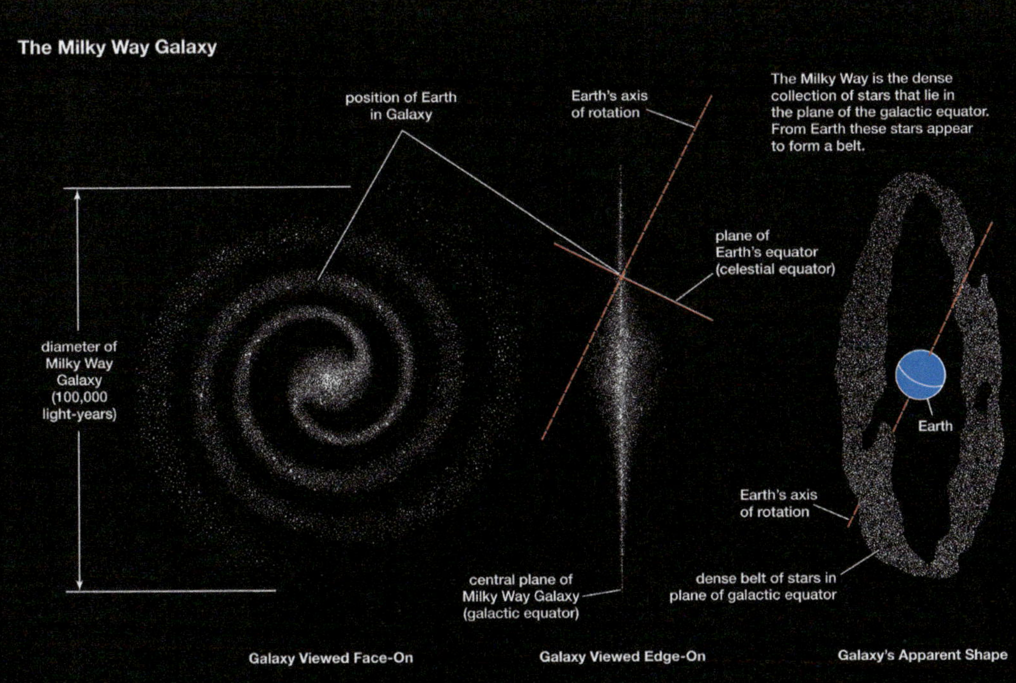

Three views of the Milky Way Galaxy.

all, of the O-type stars were formed and still exist in clusters and associations. Though only 10 percent of the total number of B-type stars are now in OB associations or clusters, it is likely that all formed in them. At the other (fainter) end of the range of stellar luminosities, the number of dwarf variable stars in the nearby T associations is estimated at 12,000. These associations are apparently the main source of low-luminosity stars in the neighbourhood of the Sun.

While large numbers of associations have formed and dispersed and provided a population of stars for the spiral arms, the globular clusters have survived relatively unchanged except for the evolutionary differences that time brings. They are too massive to be disrupted by the tidal forces of the Galaxy, though their limiting dimensions are set by these forces when they most closely approach the galactic centre. Impressive as they are individually, their total mass of 10 million suns is small compared with the mass of the Galaxy as a whole—only about 1/10,000. Their substance is that of the Galaxy in a very early stage. The Galaxy probably collapsed from a gaseous cloud composed almost entirely of hydrogen and helium. About 13.5 billion years ago, before the last stages of the collapse, matter forming the globular clusters may have separated from the rest. The fact that metal-rich clusters are near the galactic nucleus while metal-poor clusters are in the halo or outer fringes may indicate a nonuniform distribution of elements throughout the primordial mass. However, there is evidence that galaxies are given to cannibalism, in which smaller galaxies merge with larger ones that do not necessarily have the same properties. This has complicated the picture of chemical evolution. The case of the globular cluster Omega Centauri suggests this merging also may happen on smaller scales. Its stars are unusual, perhaps unique, in having a variety of chemical compositions, as though they came from more than one earlier cluster.

In a study of star clusters, a time panorama unfolds—from the oldest objects existing in the Galaxy, the globular clusters, through clusters in existence only half as long, to extremely young open clusters and associations that have come into being since humans first trod Earth.

FINDING CLUSTERS IN EXTERNAL GALAXIES

Clusters have been discovered and studied in many external galaxies, particularly members of the Local Group (a group of about 50 stellar systems to which the Galaxy belongs). At their great distances classification is difficult, but it has been accomplished from studies of the colours of the light from an entire cluster (integrated colours) or, for relatively few, from colour-magnitude diagrams.

Infant stars in the Small Magellanic Cloud.

Clusters have been found by the hundreds in some of the nearest galaxies. At the distance of the Magellanic Clouds, a cluster like the Pleiades would appear as a faint 15th-magnitude object, subtending 15 seconds of arc instead of several degrees. Nevertheless, it is estimated that the Small Magellanic Cloud, at a distance of 200,000 light-years, contains about 2,000 open clusters. In the Large Magellanic Cloud, at a distance of 163,000 light-years, over 1,200 of an estimated 4,200 have been cataloged. Most of them are young blue-giant open clusters such as NGC 330 and NGC 1866. The open clusters contain some Cepheid variables and in chemical composition are similar to, but not exactly the same as, those of the Galaxy. The globular clusters fall into two distinct groups. Those of the first group, the red, have a large metal deficiency similar to the globular clusters in the Galaxy, and some are known to contain RR Lyrae variables. The globular clusters of the second group are large and circular in outline, with colours much bluer than normal galactic globular clusters and with ages of about one million to one billion years. They are similar to the open clusters of the Magellanic Clouds but are very populous. The observed differences between clusters in the Galaxy and the Magellanic Clouds result from small differences in helium or heavy-element abundances. There are at least 122 associations with a mean diameter of 250 light-years, somewhat richer and larger than in the Galaxy.

Sixteen of the associations contain coexistent clusters. Also, 15 star clouds (aggregations of many thousands of stars dispersed over hundreds or even thousands of light-years) are recognized.

In the great Andromeda spiral galaxy (M31) some 2.2 million light-years away, about 400 globular clusters are known. Colour studies of some of these clusters reveal that they have a higher metal content than globular clusters of the galaxy. Nearly 200 OB associations are known, with distances up to 80,000 light-years from the nucleus. The diameters of their dense cores are comparable to those of galactic associations. NGC 206 (OB 78) is the richest star cloud in M31, having a total mass of 200,000 suns and bearing a strong resemblance to the double cluster in Perseus. Some globular clusters have been found around the dwarf elliptical companions to M31, NGC 185, and NGC 205.

M33 in the constellation Triangulum—a spiral galaxy with thick, loose arms (an Sc system in the Hubble classification scheme)—has about 300 known clusters, not many of which have globular characteristics. Of the six dwarf spheroidal galaxies in the Local Group, only the one in the constellation Fornax has clusters. Its five globular clusters are similar to the bluest globular clusters of the galaxy. No clusters have been discovered in the irregular galaxies NGC 6822 and IC 1613.

Beyond the Local Group, at a distance of 45 million light-years, the giant elliptical galaxy M87 in the Virgo cluster of galaxies is surrounded by an estimated 13,000 globular star clusters. Inspection of other elliptical galaxies in Virgo shows that they too have globular clusters whose apparent magnitudes are similar to those in M87, though their stellar population is substantially smaller. It appears that the mean absolute magnitudes of globular clusters are constant and independent of the absolute luminosity of the parent galaxy.

The total number of clusters now known in external galaxies far exceeds the number known in the Milky Way system.

CHAPTER 3

SUPER STARS

The final stages in the evolution of a star depend on its mass and angular momentum and whether it is a member of a close binary. Stars about 10 times the Sun's mass pass through the hydrogen-to-helium fusion process almost 5,000 times faster. These stars swell to red supergiants only a few million years after birth. They then go through multiple pulsations, as they fuse heavier and heavier elements for energy to fight off the crush of gravity. Finally, an ultradense core of almost pure iron, at temperatures of billions of kelvins, begins to form. After only a day, this core reaches a mass 1.4 times that of the Sun. In a fraction of a second, almost all of the roughly 10^{57} protons and 10^{57} electrons in the core combine to form neutrons, robbing the core of the electron degeneracy pressure that had been preventing its collapse.

The collapse now ensues at a large fraction of the speed of light, crushing the core to a phenomenal density of 10^{14} times that of water. An effect of quantum mechanics called neutron degeneracy suddenly halts the collapse of the core when it has shrunk to about 10 miles (16 kilometers) in diameter. The core rebounds, however. This sends a titanic shock wave out through the vast surrounding layers of the star, which explode as a supernova.

Such an exploding star releases as much light as billions of main-sequence stars. It shines like this for weeks as the materials spread out into space at tens of thousands of miles per second. The expanding debris can then be incorporated into other nebulae (perhaps also triggering their collapse) and ultimately new stars and planets. In fact, most astronomers think that the elements heavier than helium that make up Earth and its inhabitants were mainly forged in stars and distributed by one or more such ancient stellar explosions.

The tiny core of the star remains after the collision. This object, with roughly the mass of the Sun and a diameter of only about 12 miles (20 kilometers), is called a neutron star. Neutron stars generally spin rapidly, and some have strong magnetic fields that focus emitted radiation in beams. If such a beam happens to intercept Earth, observers see the star apparently flashing on and off—sometimes hundreds of times per second. The object is then called a pulsar.

Even more massive stars, with perhaps 30 or more times the mass of the Sun, face an even more extreme fate.

After reaching the red supergiant stage and producing an iron core, so much mass—at least 2 or 3 times that of the Sun—remains in the core that nothing can stop the crush of gravity. The collapsing star's gravity becomes so strong that even light cannot escape it, so it is called a black hole.

WHITE DWARFS

The faint white dwarf stars represent the endpoint of the evolution of intermediate-and low-mass stars. White dwarf stars, so called because of the white colour of the first few that were discovered, are characterized by a low luminosity, a mass on the order of that of the Sun, and a radius comparable to that of Earth. Because of their large mass and small dimensions, such stars are dense and compact objects with average densities approaching 1,000,000 times that of water.

Unlike most other stars that are supported against their own gravitation by normal gas pressure, white dwarf stars are supported by the degeneracy pressure of the electron gas in their interior. Degeneracy pressure is the increased resistance exerted by electrons composing the gas, as a result of stellar contraction.

The central region of a typical white dwarf star is composed of a mixture of carbon and oxygen. Surrounding this core is a thin envelope of helium and, in most cases, an even thinner layer of hydrogen. A very few white dwarf stars are surrounded by a thin carbon envelope. Only the outermost stellar layers are accessible to astronomical observations.

White dwarfs evolve from stars with an initial mass of up to three or four solar masses or even possibly higher. After quiescent phases of hydrogen and helium burning in its core—separated by a first red-giant phase—the star becomes a red giant for a second time. Near the end of this second red-giant phase, the star loses its extended envelope in a catastrophic event, leaving behind a dense, hot, and luminous core surrounded by a glowing spherical shell. This is the planetary-nebula phase. During the entire course of its evolution, which typically takes several billion years, the star will lose a major fraction of its original mass through stellar winds in the giant phases and through its ejected envelope. The hot planetary-nebula nucleus left behind has a mass of 0.5–1.0 solar mass and will eventually cool down to become a white dwarf.

White dwarfs have exhausted all their nuclear fuel and so have no residual nuclear energy sources. Their compact structure also prevents further gravitational contraction. The energy radiated away into the interstellar medium is thus provided by the residual thermal energy of the nondegenerate ions composing its core. That energy slowly diffuses outward through the insulating stellar envelope, and the white dwarf slowly cools down. Following the complete exhaustion of this reservoir of thermal energy, a process that takes several additional billion years, the white dwarf stops radiating and has by then reached the final stage of its evolution and becomes a cold and inert stellar remnant. Such an object is sometimes called a black dwarf.

White dwarf stars are occasionally found in binary systems, as is the case for the white dwarf companion to the brightest star in the night sky, Sirius. Aside from playing an essential role in Type Ia supernovae, they are also behind the outbursts of novae and of other cataclysmic variable stars. Novae are a class of exploding stars whose luminosity temporarily increases from several thousand to as much as 100,000 times its normal level. A nova reaches maximum luminosity within hours after its outburst and may shine intensely for several days or occasionally for a few weeks, after which it slowly returns to its former level of luminosity. Stars that become novae are nearly always too faint before eruption to be seen with the unaided eye. Their sudden increase in luminosity, however, is sometimes great enough to make them readily visible in the nighttime sky. To observers, such objects may appear to be new stars; hence the name nova from the Latin word for "new."

Most novae are thought to occur in double-star systems in which members revolve closely around each other. Both members of such a system, commonly called a close binary star, are aged: one is a red giant and the other a white dwarf. In certain cases, the red giant expands into the gravitational domain of its companion. The gravitational field of the white dwarf is so strong that hydrogen-rich matter from the outer atmosphere of the red giant is pulled onto the smaller star. When a sizable quantity of this material accumulates on the surface of the white dwarf, a nuclear explosion occurs there, causing the ejection of hot surface gases on the order of 1/10,000 the amount of material in the Sun. According to the prevailing theory, the white dwarf settles down after the explosion; however, the flow of hydrogen-rich material resumes immediately, and the whole process that produced the outburst repeats itself, resulting in another explosion about 1,000 to 10,000 years later. Recent research, however, suggests that such outbursts may recur at much longer intervals—every 100,000 years or so. It is explained that a nova eruption separates the members of the binary system, interrupting the transfer of matter until the two stars move close together again after a considerable length of time.

NEUTRON STARS

When the mass of a star's remnant core lies between 1.4 and about 2 solar masses, it apparently becomes a neutron star with a density more than a million times greater than even that of a white dwarf. These extremely dense, compact stars are thought to be composed primarily of neutrons. Neutron stars are typically about 20 km (12 miles) in diameter. Their masses range between 1.18 and 1.44 times that of the Sun, but most are 1.35 times that of the Sun. Thus, their mean densities are extremely high—about 10^{14} times that of water. This approximates the density inside the atomic nucleus, and in some ways a neutron star can be conceived of as a gigantic nucleus.

It is not known definitively what is at the centre of the star, where the pressure is greatest; theories include hyperons, kaons, pions, and strange quark matter. The intermediate layers are mostly neutrons and are probably in a "superfluid" state. The outer 1 km (0.6 mile) is solid, in spite of the high temperatures, which can be as high as 1,000,000 K. The surface of this solid layer, where the pressure is lowest, is composed of an extremely dense form of iron.

Another important characteristic of neutron stars is the presence of very strong magnetic fields, upwards of 10^{12} Gauss (Earth's magnetic field is 0.5 Gauss), which causes the surface iron to be polymerized in the form of long chains of iron atoms. The individual atoms become compressed and elongated in the direction of the magnetic field and can bind together end-to-end. Below the surface, the pressure becomes much too high for individual atoms to exist.

The discovery of pulsars provided the first evidence of the existence of neutron stars. Pulsars are neutron stars that emit pulses of radiation once per rotation. The radiation emitted is usually radio waves. However, some objects are known to give off short rhythmic bursts of visible light, X-rays, and gamma radiation as well, and

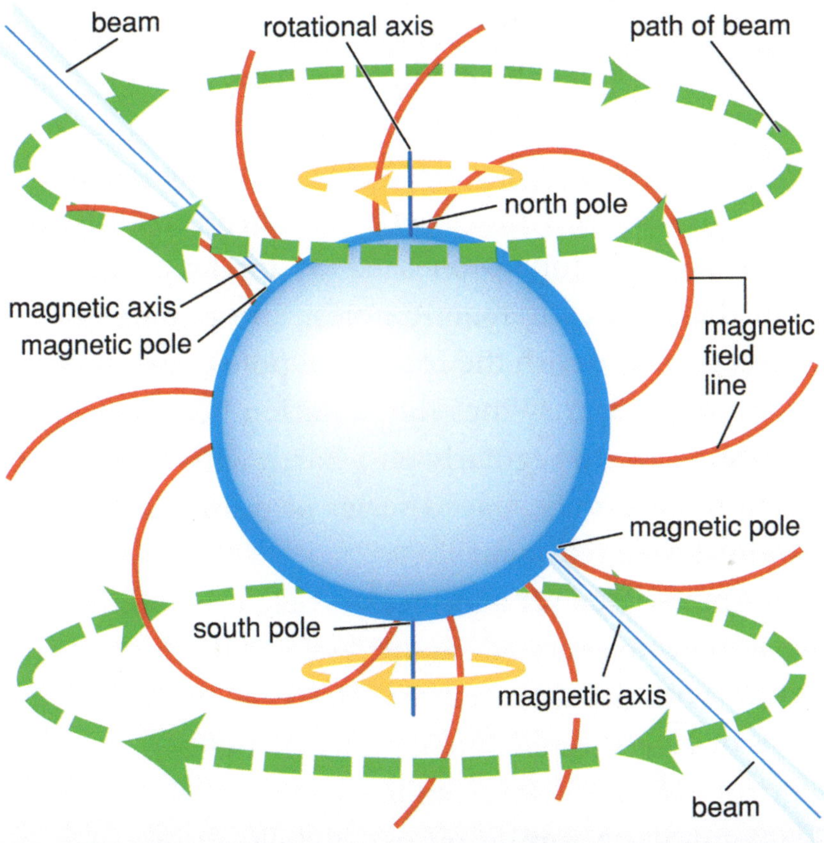

If the magnetic axis of a pulsar is offset from the rotational axis, as the star rotates, the beams of electromagnetic radiation will sweep out circular paths.

others are "radio-quiet" and emit only at X- or gamma-ray wavelengths. The very short periods of, for example, the Crab (NP 0532) and Vela pulsars (33 and 83 milliseconds, respectively) rule out the possibility that they might be white dwarfs. The pulses result from electrodynamic phenomena generated by their rotation and their strong magnetic fields, as in a dynamo. In the case of radio pulsars, neutrons at the surface of the star decay into protons and electrons. As these charged particles are released from the surface, they enter the intense magnetic field (10^{12} Gauss) that surrounds the star and rotates along with it. Accelerated to speeds approaching that of light, the particles give off electromagnetic radiation by synchrotron emission.

This radiation is released as intense radio beams from the pulsar's magnetic poles. These magnetic poles do not coincide with the rotational poles, and so the rotation of the pulsar swings the radiation beams around. As the beams sweep regularly past Earth with each complete rotation, an evenly spaced series of pulses is detected by ground-based telescopes.

Antony Hewish and Jocelyn Bell, astronomers working at the University of Cambridge, first discovered pulsars in 1967 with the aid of a radio telescope specially designed to record very rapid fluctuations in radio sources. Subsequent searches have resulted in the detection of about 2,000 pulsars. A significant percentage of these objects are

MAIN PULSE   "OFF" PHASE

PULSAR IN THE CRAB NEBULA

Two X-ray images of the Crab Pulsar (NP 0532), thought to be the collapsed remnant of a supernova, discovered near the centre of the Crab Nebula.

concentrated toward the plane of the Milky Way Galaxy, the enormous galactic system in which Earth is located.

Although all known pulsars exhibit similar behaviour, they show considerable variation in the length of their periods—i.e., the intervals between successive pulses. The period of the slowest pulsar so far observed is about 11.8 seconds in duration. The pulsar designated PSR J1939+2134 was the fastest-known for more than two decades. Discovered in 1982, it has a period of 0.00155 second, or 1.55 milliseconds, which means it is spinning 642 times per second. In 2006 an even faster one was reported; known as J1748–2446ad, it has a period of 1.396 milliseconds, which corresponds to a spin rate of 716 times per second. These spin rates are close to the theoretical limit for a pulsar because a neutron star rotating only about four times faster would fly apart as a result of "centrifugal force" at its equator, notwithstanding a gravitational pull so strong that the star's escape velocity is about half the speed of light.

These fast pulsars are known as millisecond pulsars. They form in supernovae like slower rotating pulsars; however, millisecond pulsars often occur in binary star systems. After the supernova, the neutron star accretes matter from its companion, causing the pulsar to spin faster.

Careful timing of radio pulsars shows that they are slowing down very gradually at a rate of typically a millionth of a second per year. The ratio of a pulsar's present period to the average slow-down rate gives some indication of its age. This so-called characteristic, or timing, age can be in close agreement with the actual age. For example, the Crab Pulsar, which was formed during a supernova explosion observed in 1054 CE, has a characteristic age of 1,240 years; however, pulsar J0205+6449, which was formed during a supernova in 1181 CE, has a characteristic age of 5,390 years.

Because pulsars slow down so gradually, they are very accurate clocks. Since pulsars also have strong gravitational fields, this accuracy can be used to test theories of gravity.

American physicists Joseph Taylor and Russell Hulse won the Nobel Prize for Physics in 1993 for their study of timing variations in the pulsar PSR 1913+16. PSR 1913+16 has a companion neutron star with which it is locked in a tight orbit. The two stars' enormous interacting gravitational fields affect the regularity of the radio pulses, and by timing these and analyzing their variations, Taylor and Hulse found that the stars were rotating ever faster around each other in an increasingly tight orbit. This orbital decay is presumed to occur because the system is losing energy in the form of gravity waves. This was the first experimental evidence for the existence of the gravitational waves predicted by Albert Einstein in his general theory of relativity.

Some pulsars, such as the Crab and Vela pulsars, are losing rotational energy so precipitously that they also emit radiation of shorter wavelength. The Crab Pulsar appears in optical photographs as a moderately bright (magnitude 16) star in the centre of the Crab Nebula. Soon after the detection of its radio pulses in 1968, astronomers at the Steward Observatory in Arizona found that visible light from the Crab Pulsar flashes at exactly the same rate. The star also produces regular pulses of X-rays and gamma rays.

The Vela Pulsar is much fainter at optical wavelengths (average magnitude 24) and was observed in 1977 during a particularly sensitive search with the large

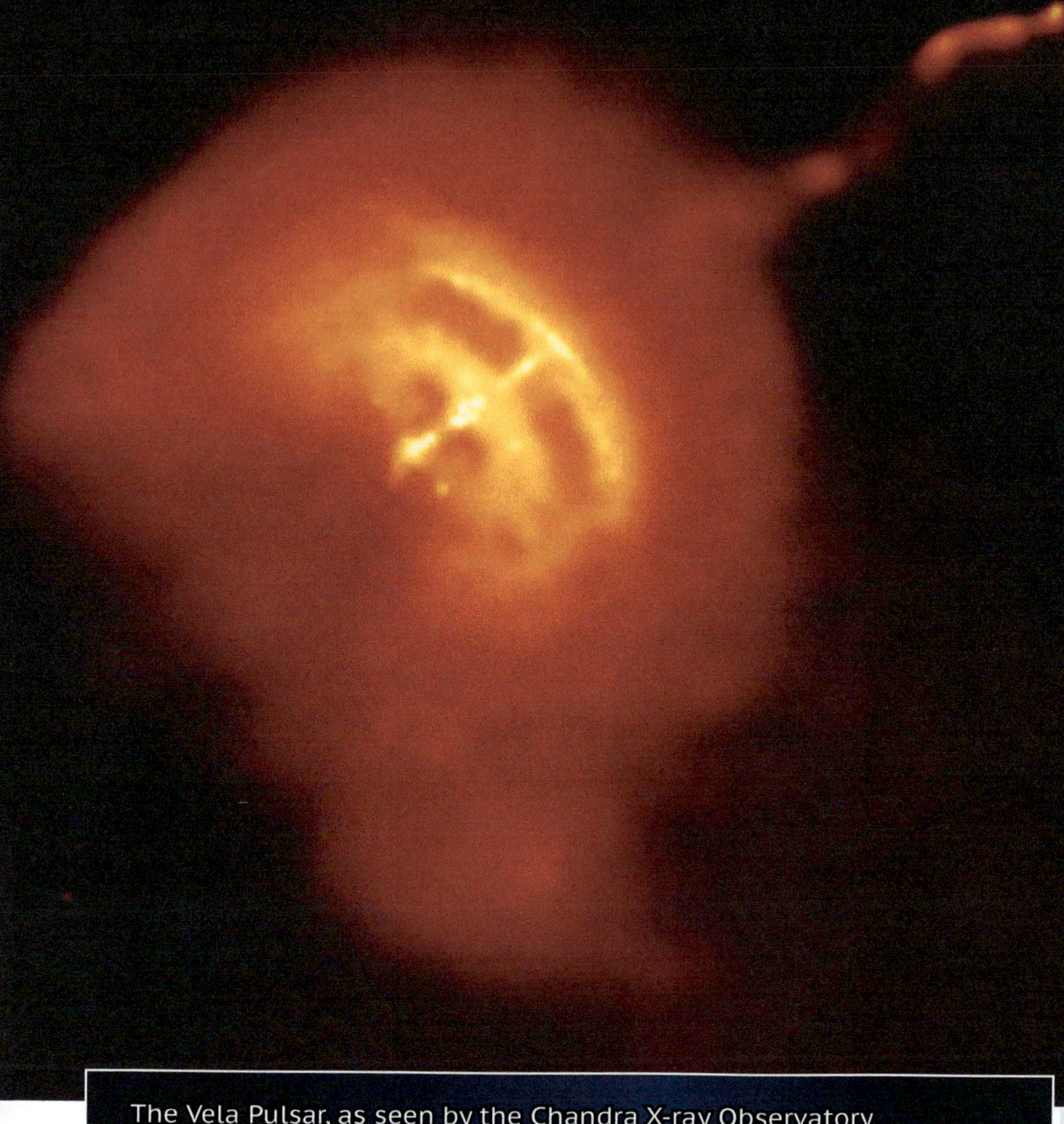

Anglo-Australian Telescope situated at Parkes, Australia. It also pulses at X-ray wavelengths. The Vela Pulsar does, however, give off gamma rays in regular pulses and is the most intense source of such radiation in the sky.

Pulsars also experience much more drastic period changes, which are called glitches, in which the period suddenly increases and then gradually decreases to its pre-glitch value. Some glitches are caused by "starquakes," or sudden cracks in the rigid iron crust of the star. Others are caused by an interaction between the crust and the more fluid interior. Usually the interior is loosely coupled to the crust, so the crust can slow down relative to the interior. However, sometimes the coupling between the crust and interior becomes stronger, spinning up the pulsar and causing a glitch.

Some X-ray pulsars are "accreting" pulsars. These pulsars are in binaries; the neutron star accretes material from its companion. This material flows to the magnetic polar caps, where it releases X-rays. Another class of X-ray pulsars is called "anomalous." These pulsars have periods of more than five seconds, sometimes give off bursts of X-rays, and are often associated with supernova remnants. These pulsars arise from highly magnetized neutron stars, or magnetars, which have a magnetic field of between 10^{14} and 10^{15} Gauss. (The magnetars also have been identified with another class of objects, the soft gamma-ray repeaters, which give off bursts of gamma rays.)

Some pulsars emit only in gamma rays. In 2008 the Fermi Gamma-ray Space Telescope discovered the first such pulsar within the supernova remnant CTA 1; since then, it has found over 200 others. Unlike radio pulsars, the gamma-ray emission does not come from the particle beams at the poles but arises far from the neutron star surface. The precise physical process that generates the gamma-ray pulses is unknown.

Many binary X-ray sources, such as Hercules X-1, contain neutron stars. Cosmic objects of this kind emit X-rays by compression of material from companion stars accreted onto their surfaces.

Neutron stars are also seen as objects called rotating radio transients (RRATs) and as magnetars. The RRATs are sources that emit single radio bursts but at irregular intervals ranging from four minutes to three hours. The cause of the RRAT phenomenon is unknown. Magnetars are highly magnetized neutron stars that have a magnetic field of between 10^{14} and 10^{15} Gauss.

Most investigators believe that neutron stars are formed by supernova explosions in which the collapse of the central core of the supernova is halted by rising neutron pressure as the core density increases to about 10^{15} grams per cubic cm. If the collapsing core is more massive than about three solar masses, however, a neutron star cannot be formed, and the core would presumably become a black hole.

BLACK HOLES

A black hole can be formed by the death of a massive star that exceeds about two solar masses. When such a star has exhausted its internal thermonuclear fuels at the end of its life, it becomes unstable and gravitationally collapses inward upon itself. The crushing weight of constituent matter falling in from all sides compresses the dying star to a point of zero volume and infinite density called the singularity. Details of the structure of a black hole are calculated from Albert Einstein's general theory of relativity. The singularity constitutes the centre of a black hole and is hidden by the object's "surface," the event horizon. Inside the event horizon the escape velocity (i.e., the velocity required for matter to escape from the gravitational field of a cosmic object) exceeds the speed of light, so that not even rays of light can escape into space.

The radius of the event horizon is called the Schwarzschild radius, after the German astronomer Karl Schwarzschild, who in 1916 predicted the existence of collapsed stellar bodies that emit no radiation. The Schwarzschild radius (R_g) of an object of mass M is given by the following formula, in which G is the universal gravitational constant and c is the speed of light:

$$R_g = 2GM/c^2$$

The size of the Schwarzschild radius is proportional to the mass of the collapsing star. For a black hole with a

STEPHEN HAWKING'S WORK ON BLACK HOLES

Stephen William Hawking (1942–2018) was a theoretical physicist whose theory of exploding black holes drew upon both relativity theory and quantum mechanics. He also worked with space-time singularities.

Hawking studied physics at University College, Oxford (B.A., 1962), and Trinity Hall, Cambridge (Ph.D., 1966). He was elected a research fellow at Gonville and Caius College at Cambridge. In the early 1960s Hawking contracted amyotrophic lateral sclerosis, an incurable degenerative neuromuscular disease. He continued to work despite the disease's progressively disabling effects.

Hawking worked primarily in the field of general relativity and particularly on the physics of black holes. In 1971 he suggested the formation, following the big bang, of numerous objects containing as much as one billion tons of mass but occupying only the space of a proton. These objects, called mini black holes, are unique in that their immense mass and gravity require that they be ruled by the laws of relativity, while their minute size requires that the laws of quantum mechanics apply to them also.

In 1974 Hawking proposed that, in accordance with the predictions of quantum theory, black holes emit subatomic particles until they exhaust their energy and finally explode. Hawking's work greatly spurred efforts to theoretically delineate the properties of black holes, objects about which it was previously thought that nothing could be known. His work was also important because it showed these properties' relationship to the laws of classical thermodynamics and quantum mechanics.

mass 10 times as great as that of the Sun, the radius would be 30 km (18.6 miles).

Black holes cannot be observed directly on account of both their small size and the fact that they emit no light. They can be "observed," however, by the effects of their enormous gravitational fields on nearby matter. For example, if a black hole is a member of a binary star system, matter flowing into it from its companion becomes intensely heated and then radiates X-rays copiously before entering the event horizon of the black hole and disappearing forever. One of the component stars of the binary X-ray system Cygnus X-1 is a black hole. Discovered in 1971 in the constellation Cygnus, this binary consists of a blue supergiant and an invisible companion 8.7 times the mass of the Sun that revolve about one another in a period of 5.6 days.

Some black holes apparently have nonstellar origins. Various astronomers have speculated that large volumes of interstellar gas collect and collapse into supermassive black holes at the centres of quasars and galaxies. A mass of gas falling rapidly into a black hole is estimated to give off more than 100 times as much energy as is released by the identical amount of mass through nuclear fusion. Accordingly, the collapse of millions or billions of solar masses of interstellar gas under gravitational force into a large black hole would account for the enormous energy output of quasars and certain galactic systems. One such supermassive black hole, Sagittarius A*, exists at the centre of the Milky Way Galaxy. In 2005, infrared observations of stars orbiting around the position of Sagittarius A* demonstrated the presence of a black hole with a mass equivalent to 4,310,000 Suns.

Supermassive black holes have been seen in other galaxies as well. In 1994 the Hubble Space Telescope provided conclusive evidence for the existence of a supermassive black hole at the centre of the M87 galaxy. It has a mass equal to two to three billion Suns but is no larger than the solar system. The black hole's existence can be inferred from its energetic effects on an envelope of gas swirling around it at extremely high velocities.

Composite image of giant elliptical galaxy M87 (Virgo A). Jets moving at the speed of light are seen coming from the massive black hole at the centre of the galaxy.

The existence of another kind of nonstellar black hole was proposed by Stephen Hawking. According to Hawking's theory, numerous tiny primordial black holes, possibly with a mass equal to that of an asteroid or less, might have been created during the big bang, a state of extremely high temperatures and density in which the universe is thought to have originated 13.7 billion years ago. These mini black holes, like the more massive variety, lose mass and disappear over time through Hawking radiation, which is radiation theoretically emitted from just outside the event horizon of a black hole.

CHAPTER 4

NEBULAE

In between the stars are light-years of seemingly empty space. However, these regions are in fact occupied by clouds of dust and gas called nebulae. This dust and gas originate from the remnants of stars, and from this material, new ones are born.

Nebulae are any of the various tenuous clouds of gas and dust that occur in interstellar space. The term *nebula* was formerly applied to any object outside the solar system that had a diffuse appearance rather than a pointlike image, as in the case of a star. This definition, adopted at a time when very distant objects could not be resolved into great detail, unfortunately includes two unrelated classes of objects: the extragalactic nebulae, now called galaxies, which are enormous collections of stars and gas, and the galactic nebulae, which are composed of the interstellar medium (the gas between the stars, with its accompanying small solid particles) within a single galaxy. Today the term *nebula* generally refers exclusively to the interstellar medium.

The Cat's Eye nebula.

In a spiral galaxy the interstellar medium makes up 3 to 5 percent of the galaxy's mass, but within a spiral arm its mass fraction increases to about 20 percent. About 1 percent of the mass of the interstellar medium is in the form of "dust"—small solid particles that are efficient in absorbing and scattering radiation. Much of the rest of the mass within a galaxy is concentrated in visible stars, but there is also some form of dark matter that accounts for a substantial fraction of the mass in the outer regions.

The most conspicuous property of interstellar gas is its clumpy distribution on all size scales observed, from the size of the entire Milky Way Galaxy (about 10^{20} metres, or hundreds of thousands of light-years) down to the distance from Earth to the Sun (about 10^{11} metres, or a few light-minutes). The large-scale variations are seen by direct observation; the small-scale variations are observed by fluctuations in the intensity of radio waves, similar to the "twinkling" of starlight caused by unsteadiness in the Earth's atmosphere. Various regions exhibit an enormous range of densities and temperatures. Within the Galaxy's spiral arms about half the mass of the interstellar medium is concentrated in molecular clouds, in which hydrogen occurs in molecular form (H_2) and temperatures are as low as 10 kelvins (K). These clouds are inconspicuous optically and are detected principally by their carbon monoxide (CO) emissions in the millimetre wavelength range.

Their densities in the regions studied by CO emissions are typically 1,000 H_2 molecules per cubic cm. At the other extreme is the gas between the clouds, with a temperature of 10 million K and a density of only 0.001 H^+ ion per cubic cm. Such gas is produced by supernovae, the violent explosions of unstable stars.

THE DIFFERENT CLASSES OF NEBULAE

All nebulae observed in the Milky Way Galaxy are forms of interstellar matter—namely, the gas between the stars that is almost always accompanied by solid grains of cosmic dust. Their appearance differs widely, depending not only on the temperature and density of the material observed but also on how the material is spatially situated with respect to the observer. Their chemical composition, however, is fairly uniform; it corresponds to the composition of the universe in general in that approximately 90 percent of the constituent atoms are hydrogen and nearly all the rest are helium, with oxygen, carbon, neon, nitrogen, and the other elements together making up about two atoms per thousand. On the basis of appearance, nebulae can be divided into two broad classes: dark nebulae and bright nebulae. Dark nebulae appear as irregularly shaped black patches in the sky and blot out the light of the stars that lie beyond them. Bright nebulae appear as faintly luminous glowing surfaces; they either emit their own light or reflect the light of nearby stars.

Dark nebulae are very dense and cold molecular clouds; they contain about half of all interstellar material. Typical densities range from hundreds to millions (or more) of hydrogen molecules per cubic centimetre. These clouds are the sites where new stars are formed through the gravitational collapse of some of their parts. Most of the remaining gas is in the diffuse interstellar medium, relatively inconspicuous because of its very low density (about 0.1 hydrogen atom per cubic cm) but detectable by its radio emission of the 21-cm line of neutral hydrogen.

Bright nebulae are comparatively dense clouds of gas within the diffuse interstellar medium. They have several sub-classes: (1) reflection nebulae, (2) H II regions, (3) diffuse ion-ized gas, (4) planetary nebulae, and (5) supernova remnants.

Reflection nebulae reflect the light of a nearby star from their constituent dust grains. The gas of reflection nebulae is cold, and such objects would be seen as dark nebulae if it were not for the nearby light source.

H II regions are clouds of hydrogen ionized (sepa-rated into positive H^+ ions and free electrons) by a neigh-bouring hot star. The star must be of stellar type O or B, the most massive and hottest of normal stars in the Gal-axy, in order to produce enough of the radiation required to ionize the hydrogen.

Diffuse ionized gas, so pervasive among the nebular clouds, is a major component of the Galaxy. It is observed by faint emissions of positive hydrogen, nitrogen, and sulfur ions (H^+, N^+, and S^+) detectable in all directions. These emissions collectively require far more power than the much more spectacular H II regions, planetary nebulae, or supernova remnants that occupy a tiny fraction of the volume.

Planetary nebulae are ejected from stars that are dying but are not massive enough to become supernovae—namely, red giant stars. That is to say, a red giant has shed its outer envelope in a less-violent event than a

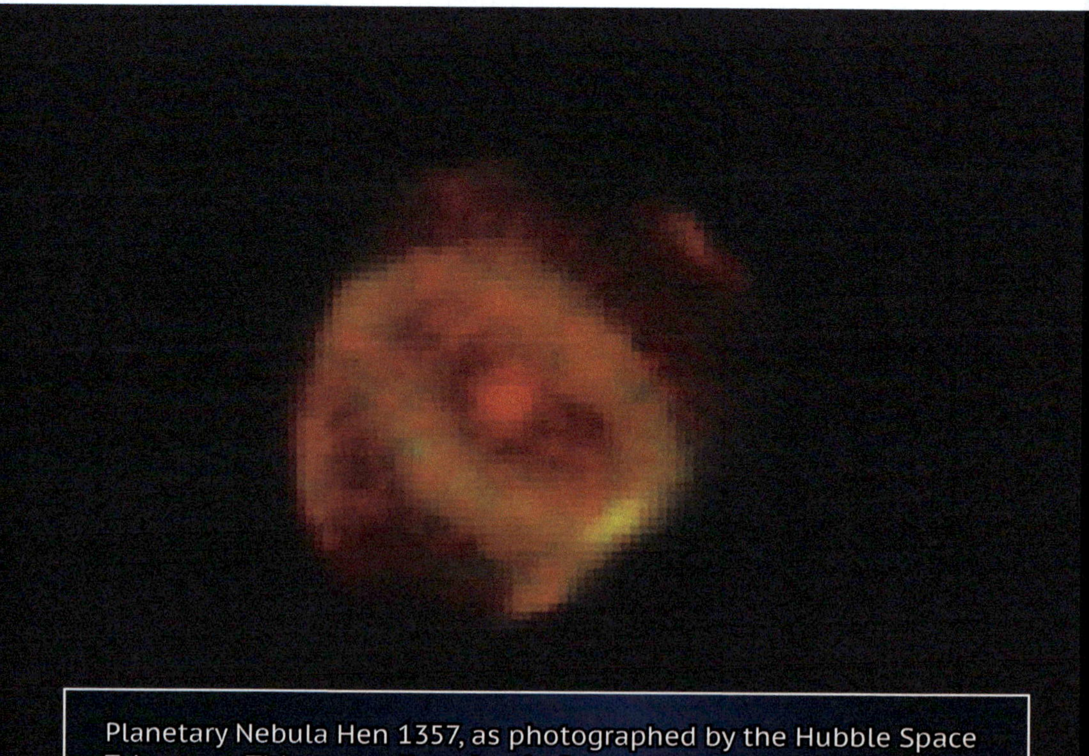

Planetary Nebula Hen 1357, as photographed by the Hubble Space Telescope. This expanding cloud of gas was expelled from an aging star in the nebula's centre.

supernova explosion and has become an intensely hot star surrounded by a shell of material that is expanding at a speed of tens of kilometres per second. Planetary nebulae typically appear as rather round objects of relatively high surface brightness. Their name is derived from their superficial resemblance to planets—i.e., their regular appearance when viewed telescopically as compared with the chaotic forms of other types of nebula.

Supernova remnants are the clouds of gas expanding at speeds of hundreds or even thousands of kilometres per second from comparatively recent explosions of massive stars. If a supernova remnant is younger than a few thousand years, it may be assumed that the gas in the nebula was mostly ejected by the exploded star. Otherwise, the nebula would consist chiefly of interstellar gas that has been swept up by the expanding remnant of older objects.

THE HISTORICAL STUDY OF NEBULAE

In 1610, two years after the invention of the telescope, the Orion Nebula, which looks like a star to the naked eye, was discovered by the French scholar and naturalist Nicolas-Claude Fabri de Peiresc. In 1656 Christiaan Huygens, the Dutch scholar and scientist, using his own greatly superior instruments, was the first to describe the bright inner region of the nebula and to determine that its inner

A star-forming region in the Orion Nebula (M42, NGC 1976).

star is not single but a compact quadruple system.

Early 18th-century observational astronomers gave high priority to comet seeking. A by-product of their search was the discovery of many bright nebulae. Several catalogs of special objects were compiled by comet researchers; by far the best known is that of the Frenchman Charles Messier, who in 1781 compiled a catalog of 103 nebulous, or extended, objects in order to prevent their confusion with comets. Most are clusters of stars, 35 are galaxies, and 11 are nebulae. Even today many of these objects are commonly referred to by their Messier catalog number; M20, for instance, is the great Trifid Nebula, in the constellation Sagittarius.

THE WORK OF THE HERSCHELS

By far the greatest observers of the early and middle 19th century were the English astronomers William Herschel and his son John. Between 1786 and 1802 William Herschel, aided by his sister Caroline, compiled three catalogs totaling about 2,500 clusters, nebulae, and galaxies. John Herschel later added to the catalogs 1,700 other nebulous objects in the southern sky visible from the Cape Observatory in South Africa but not from London and 500 more objects in the northern sky visible from England.

The catalogs of the Herschels formed the basis for the great *New General Catalogue (NGC)* of J.L. Dreyer, published in 1888. It contains the location and a brief description of 7,840 nebulae, galaxies, and clusters. In 1895 and 1908 it was supplemented by two *Index Catalogues (IC)* of 5,386 additional objects. The list still included galaxies as well as true nebulae, for they were often at this time still indistinguishable. Most of the brighter galaxies are still identified by their NGC or IC numbers according to their listing in the *New General Catalogue* or *Index Catalogues.*

The 20th century witnessed enormous advances in observational techniques as well as in the scientific understanding of the physical processes that operate in interstellar matter. In 1930 a German optical worker, Bernhard Schmidt, invented an extremely fast wide-angled camera

Engraved portrait of German-born British astronomer William Herschel, early 19th century.

ideal for photographing faint extended nebulae. Photographic plates became progressively more sensitive to an ever-widening range of colours, but photography has been completely replaced by photoelectric devices. Most images are now recorded with so-called charge-coupled devices (CCDs) that act as arrays of tiny photoelectric cells, each recording the light from a small patch of sky. Modern CCDs consist of square arrays of up to 4,000 cells on each side, or 16 million independent photocells, capable of observing the sky simultaneously. Electronic detectors are up to 100 times more sensitive than photography, can record a much wider range of light levels, and are sensitive to a much wider range of wavelengths, from 0.1 micrometre in the ultraviolet (accessible only from satellites orbiting above Earth's atmosphere) to more than 1.2 micrometres in the infrared.

Spacecraft allow the observation of radiation normally absorbed by Earth's atmosphere: gamma and X-rays (which have very short wavelengths), far-ultraviolet radiation (with wavelengths shorter than about 0.3 micrometre, below which atmospheric ozone is strongly absorbing), and infrared (from about 3 micrometres to 1 mm), strongly absorbed by atmospheric water vapour and carbon dioxide. Gamma rays, X-rays, and ultraviolet radiation reveal the physical conditions in the hottest regions in space (extending to some 100 million kelvins in shocked supernova gas). Infrared radiation reveals the conditions within dark cold molecular clouds, into which starlight cannot penetrate because of absorbing dust layers.

The primary means of studying nebulae is not by images but by spectra, which show the relative distribution

Portrait of John Herschel as a young man.

STUDYING NEBULAE WITH PHOTOGRAPHY AND SPECTROSCOPY

The advent of photography, which allows the recording of faint details invisible to the naked eye and provides a permanent record of the observation for study of fine details at leisure, caused a revolution in the understanding of nebulae. In 1880 the first photograph of the Orion Nebula was made, but really good ones were not obtained until 1883. These early photographs showed a wealth of detail extending out to distances unsuspected by visual observers.

Much can be learned about the physical nature of an astronomical object by studying its spectrum—i.e., the resolution of its light into different wavelengths (or colours). Study of the spectrum of an object provides a decisive test as to whether it is composed of unresolved stars (as are galaxies) or glowing gas. Stars radiate at all wavelengths, almost always with dark absorption lines superimposed, while hot, transparent gas clouds radiate only emission lines at certain wavelengths characteristic of their constituent gases. In 1864 observation of the spectrum of the Orion Nebula showed bright emission lines of glowing gases, with conspicuous hydrogen lines and some green lines even brighter.

Early photograph taken of the Orion Nebula, circa 1882.

(CONTINUED ON THE NEXT PAGE)

(CONTINUED FROM THE PREVIOUS PAGE)

By contrast, the spectrum of galaxies was found to be stellar, so a distinction between galaxies and nebulae—that nebulae are gaseous and galaxies are stellar—was appreciated at this time, although the true sizes and distances of galaxies were not demonstrated until the 20th century.

of the radiation among various wavelengths (or colours for optical radiation). Spectra can be obtained by means of prisms (as in the earlier part of the 20th century), diffraction gratings, or crystals, in the case of X-rays. A particularly useful instrument is the echelle spectrograph, in which one coarsely ruled grating spreads the electromagnetic radiation in one direction, while another finely ruled grating disperses it in the perpendicular direction. This device, often used both in spacecraft and on the ground, allows astronomers to record simultaneously a wide range of wavelengths with very high spectral resolution (i.e., to distinguish slightly differing wavelengths). For even higher spectral resolution astronomers employ Fabry-Pérot interferometers. Spectra provide powerful diagnostics of the physical conditions within nebulae. Images and spectra provided by Earth-orbiting satellites, especially the Hubble Space Telescope, have yielded data of unprecedented quality.

Ground-based observations also have played a major role in recent advances in scientific understanding of nebulae. The emission of gas in the radio and submillimetre wavelength ranges provides crucial information regarding physical conditions and molecular composition. Large radio telescope arrays, in which several individual telescopes function collectively as a single enormous instrument, give spatial resolutions in the radio regime far superior to any yet achieved by optical means.

THE CHEMICAL AND PHYSICAL NATURE OF NEBULAE

Many characteristics of nebulae are determined by the physical state of their constituent hydrogen, by far the most abundant element. For historical reasons, nebulae in which hydrogen is mainly ionized (H^+) are called H II regions, or diffuse nebulae; those in which hydrogen is mainly neutral are designated H I regions; and those in which the gas is in molecular form (H_2) are referred to as molecular clouds. The distinction is important because of major differences in the radiation that is present in the various regions and consequently in the physical conditions and processes that are important. Radiation is a wave but is carried by packets called photons. Each photon has a specified wavelength and precise energy that it carries, with gamma rays (short wavelengths) carrying the most and X-rays, ultraviolet, optical, infrared, microwave, and radio waves following in order of decreasing energies (or increasing wavelengths). Neutral hydrogen atoms are extremely efficient at absorbing ionizing radiation—that is, an energy per photon of at least 13.6 electron volts (or, equivalently, a wavelength of less than 0.0912 micrometre). If the hydrogen is mainly neutral, no radiation with energy above this threshold can penetrate except for photons with energies in the X-ray range and above (thousands of electron volts or more), in which case the hydrogen becomes somewhat transparent. The absorption by neutral hydrogen abruptly reduces the radiation field to almost zero for energies above 13.6 electron volts. This dearth of hydrogen-ionizing radiation implies that no ions requiring more ionizing energy than hydrogen can be produced, and the ionic species of all elements are limited to the lower stages of ionization. Within H II regions, with almost all the hydrogen ionized and thereby rendered nonabsorbing, photons of all energies propagate, and ions requiring energetic radiation for their production (e.g., O^{++}) occur.

Ultraviolet photons with energies of more than 11.2 electron volts can dissociate molecular hydrogen (H_2) into two H atoms. In H I regions there are enough of these photons to prevent the amount of H_2 from becoming large, but the destruction of H_2 as fast as it forms takes its toll on the number of photons of suitable energies. Furthermore, interstellar dust is a fairly efficient absorber of photons throughout the optical and ultraviolet range. In some regions of space the number of photons with energies higher than 11.2 volts is reduced to the level where H_2 cannot be destroyed as fast as it is produced on grain surfaces. In this case, H_2 becomes the dominant form of hydrogen present. The gas is then part of a molecular cloud. The role of interstellar dust in this process is crucial because H_2 cannot be formed efficiently in the gas phase.

THE DUST OF INTERSTELLAR SPACE

Only about 0.7 percent of the mass of the interstellar medium is in the form of solid grains, but these grains have a profound effect on the physical conditions within the gas. Their main effect is to absorb stellar radiation; for photons unable to ionize hydrogen and for wavelengths outside absorption lines or bands, the dust grains are much more opaque than the gas. The dust absorption increases with photon energy, so long-wavelength radiation (radio and far-infrared) can penetrate dust freely, near-infrared rather well, and ultraviolet relatively poorly. Dark, cold molecular clouds, within which all star formation takes place, owe their existence to dust. Besides absorbing starlight, the dust acts to heat the gas under some conditions (by ejecting electrons produced by the photoelectric effect, following the absorption of a stellar photon) and to cool the gas under other conditions (because the dust can radiate energy more efficiently than the gas and so in general is colder). The largest chemical effect of dust is to provide the only site of molecular hydrogen formation on grain surfaces. It also removes some heavy elements (especially iron and silicon) that would act as coolants to the gas. The optical appearance of most nebulae is significantly modified by the obscuring effects of the dust.

The chemical composition of the gas phase of the interstellar medium alone, without regard to the solid dust, can be determined from the strength of narrow absorption lines that are produced by the gas in the spectra of background stars. Comparison of the composition of the gas with cosmic (solar) abundances shows that almost all the iron, magnesium, and silicon, much of the carbon, and only some of the oxygen and nitrogen are contained in the dust. The absorption and scattering properties of the dust reveal that the solid grains are composed partially of silicaceous material similar to terrestrial rocks, though of an amorphous rather than crystalline variety. The grains also have a carbonaceous component. The carbon dust probably occurs in at least two forms: (1) grains, either free-flying or as components of composite grains that also contain silicates, and (2) individual, freely floating aromatic hydrocarbon molecules, with a range varying from 70 to several hundred carbon atoms and some hydrogen atoms that dangle from the outer edges of the molecule or are trapped in the middle of it. It is merely convention that these molecules are referred to as dust, since the smallest may be only somewhat larger than the largest molecules observed with a radio telescope. Both of the dust components are needed to explain spectroscopic features arising from the dust. In addition, there are probably mantles of hydrocarbon on the surfaces of the grains. The size of the grains ranges from perhaps as small as 0.0003 micrometre for the tiniest hydrocarbon molecules to a substantial fraction of a micrometre; there are many more small grains than large ones.

The dust cannot be formed directly from purely gaseous material at the low densities found even in comparatively dense interstellar clouds, which would be considered an excellent laboratory vacuum. For a solid to condense, the gas density must be high enough to allow a few atoms to collide and stick together long enough to radiate away their energy to cool and form a solid. Grains are known to form in the outer atmospheres of cool supergiant stars, where the gas density is comparatively high (perhaps 10^9 times what it is in typical nebulae). The grains are then blown out of the stellar atmosphere by radiation pressure (the mechanical force of the light they absorb and scatter).

Calculations indicate that refracting materials, such as the constituents of the grains proposed here, should condense in this way.

There is clear indication that the dust is heavily modified within the interstellar medium by interactions with itself and with the interstellar gas. The absorption and scattering properties of dust show that there are many more smaller grains in the diffuse interstellar medium than in dense clouds; apparently in the dense medium the small grains have coagulated into larger ones, thereby lowering the ability of the dust to absorb radiation with short wavelengths (namely, ultraviolet, near 0.1 micrometre). The gas-phase abundances of some elements, such as iron, magnesium, and nickel, also are much lower in the dense regions than in the diffuse gas, although even in the diffuse gas most of these elements are missing from the gas and are therefore condensed into dust. These systematic interactions of gas and dust show that dust grains collide with gas atoms much more rapidly than one would expect if the dust and gas simply drifted together. There must be disturbances, probably magnetic in nature, that keep the dust and gas moving with respect to each other.

The motions of gas within nebulae of all types are clearly chaotic and complicated. There are sometimes large-scale flows, such as when a hot star forms on the outer edge of a cold, quiescent dark molecular cloud and ionizes an

H II region in its vicinity. The pressure strongly increases in the newly ionized zone, so the ionized gas flows out through the surrounding material. There are also expanding structures resembling bubbles surrounding stars that are ejecting their outer atmospheres into stellar winds.

TURBULENCE IN NEBULAE

Besides these organized flows, nebulae of all types always show chaotic motions called turbulence. This is a well-known phenomenon in gas dynamics that results when there is low viscosity in flowing fluids, so the motions become chaotic eddies that transfer kinetic and magnetic energy and momentum from large scales down to small sizes. On small-enough scales viscosity always becomes important, and the energy is converted into heat, which is kinetic energy on a molecular scale. Turbulence in nebulae has profound, but poorly understood, effects on their energy balance and pressure support.

Turbulence is observed by means of the widths of the emission or absorption lines in a nebular spectrum. No line can be precisely sharp in wavelength, because the energy levels of the atom or ion from which it arises are not precisely sharp. Actual lines are usually much broader than this intrinsic width because of the Doppler effect arising from motions of the atoms along the line of sight. The emission line of an atom is shifted to longer wavelengths if it is receding from the observer and to shorter wavelengths if it is approaching. Part of the observed broadening is easily explained by thermal motions, since v^2, the averaged squared speed, is proportional to T/m, where T is the temperature and m is the mass of the atom. Thus, hydrogen atoms move the fastest at any given temperature. Observations show that in fact hydrogen lines are broader than those of other elements but not as much as expected from thermal motions alone. Turbulence represents bulk motions, independent of the mass of the atoms. This chaotic motion of gas atoms of all masses would explain the observations. The physical question, though, is what maintains the turbulence. Why do the turbulent cascades not carry kinetic energy from large-size scales into ever-shorter-size scales and finally into heat?

The answer is that energy is continuously injected into the gases by a variety of processes. One involves strong stellar winds from hot stars, which are blown off at speeds of thousands of kilometres per second. Another arises from the violently expanding remnants of supernova explosions, which sometimes start at 20,000 km (12,000 miles) per second and gradually slow to typical cloud speeds (10 km [6 miles] per second). A third process is the occasional collision of clouds moving in the overall galactic gravitational potential. All these processes inject energy on large scales that can undergo turbulent cascading to heat.

THE GALACTIC MAGNETIC FIELD

There is a pervasive magnetic field that threads the spiral arms of the Milky Way Galaxy and extends to thousands of light-years above the galactic plane. The evidence for the existence of this field comes from radio synchrotron emission produced by very energetic electrons moving through it and from the polarization of starlight that is produced by elongated dust grains that tend to be aligned with the magnetic field. The magnetic field is very strongly coupled to the gas because it acts upon the embedded electrons, even the few in H I regions, and the electrons impart some motion of the other constituents by means of collisions. The gas and field are effectively confined to moving together, even though the gas can slip along the field freely. The field has an important influence upon the turbulence because it exerts a pressure similar to gas pressure, thereby influencing the motions of the gas. The resulting complex interactions and wave motions have been studied in extensive numerical calculations.

All scientific thinking on the nature of the universe can be traced to the distinctive geometric patterns formed by the stars in the night sky. Early nomads found that knowledge of the constellations could guide their travels, and they developed stories to help them remember the relative positions of the stars in the night sky. These stories became the mythical tales that are part of most cultures.

Today, scientists and amateur astronomers alike are discovering new stars every day. We're learning more about their composition and behaviour than ever before. Though we no longer navigate by the stars as we did in ancient times, the knowledge we have gained from them gives us greater insight into the history and nature of the universe.

The discovery of stars can also give us hope for the potential for life on other planets. Stars vary widely in size, mass, brightness, and longevity. The largest are about 100 times the mass of the Sun and about 10 times the Sun's diameter. They give off almost a million times as much light as the Sun. The Sun is ideal for life on Earth. Though there are many stars in the universe similar to the Sun, most stars would not make good substitutes. However, it is likely that there are stars in the universe that may provide the right conditions for an Earthlike planet and extraterrestrial life.

GLOSSARY

astronomical unit A unit of length used in astronomy effectively equal to the mean distance of Earth from the Sun or about 93 million miles (150 million kilometres).

Big Bang The emergence of the universe from a state of very high temperature and density.

binary stars A pair of stars in orbit around a common centre of gravity.

black hole An area in space with an intense gravitational field whose escape velocity exceeds the speed of light.

brown dwarf A celestial object that is much smaller than a normal star and has insufficient mass to sustain nuclear fusion but that is hot enough to radiate energy especially at infrared wavelengths.

dark matter Nonluminous matter not yet directly detected by astronomers that is hypothesized to exist to account for various observed gravitational effects.

density The mass of a unit volume of a material substance.

dwarf star A low-luminosity star.

eclipsing binary Two close stars moving in an orbit so placed in space in relation to Earth that the light of one can at times be hidden behind the other.

event horizon The boundary of a black hole beyond which nothing can escape from within it.

general relativity A theory published by Albert Einstein in 1915 that generalizes Einstein's theory of special relativity and states that gravity is a geometric property of space and time.

interferometer An instrument that combines light waves from two or more different optical paths and can be used to measure the angle subtended by the diameter of a star at the observer's position.

interstellar Something that is located, taking place, or traveling among the stars.

mass The property of a body that is a measure of its inertia and that is commonly taken as a measure of the amount of material it contains and causes it to have weight in a gravitational field.

nebula A mass of interstellar gas and dust.

nova A star that brightens temporarily while ejecting a shell explosively.

pulsar A celestial source of pulsating electromagnetic radiation (such as radio waves) characterized by a short relatively constant interval (such as .033 second) between pulses that is held to be a rotating neutron star.

quantum mechanics A theory of matter that is based on the concept of the possession of wave properties by elementary particles, that affords a mathematical interpretation of the structure and interactions of matter on the basis of these properties, and that incorporates within it quantum theory and the uncertainty principle.

quasar The abbreviation for quasi-stellar radio source, which emits up to 100 times as much radiation as an entire galaxy.

Schwarzschild radius The radius of the spherical boundary within which a given mass (as of a star) must collapse to become a black hole.

singularity A point or region of infinite mass density at which space and time are infinitely distorted by gravitational forces and which is held to be the final state of matter falling into a black hole.

solar mass The mass of the Sun used as a unit for the expression of the masses of other celestial objects.

solar wind Plasma continuously ejected from the Sun's surface into and through interplanetary space.

special relativity A theory published by Albert Einstein in 1905, which is based on the two postulates (1) that the speed of light in a vacuum is constant and independent of the source or observer and (2) that the mathematical forms of the laws of physics are invariant in all inertial systems and which leads to the assertion of the equivalence of mass and energy and of change in mass, dimension, and time with increased velocity.

subatomic particle A particle smaller than an atom.

thermodynamics Physics that deals with the mechanical action or relations of heat.

tidal force The effect of the stretching of a body toward the center of mass of another body due to the gradient in strength of the gravitational field.

THE NATURE OF STARS

Eric Chaisson and Steve McMillan, *Astronomy Today*, 5th ed. (2005); Neil F. Comins and William J. Kaufmann III, *Discovering the Universe*, 7th ed. (2005); and R.C. Bless, *Discovering the Cosmos* (1996), contain good introductory accounts of the properties of stars. Lawrence H. Aller, *Atoms, Stars, and Nebulae*, 3rd ed. (1991), is a semipopular work emphasizing analyses of starlight, stellar spectroscopy, and evolution. Rudolf Kippenhahn, *100 Billion Suns: The Birth, Life, and Death of the Stars* (1983, reissued 1993; originally published in German, 1980), is a readable account of stellar evolution. Donald A. Cooke, *The Life & Death of Stars* (1985), has excellent illustrations. Paul Murdin and Lesley Murdin, *Supernovae*, rev. ed. (1985), is a superlative nontechnical history. Kenneth R. Lang and Owen Gingerich (eds.), *A Source Book in Astronomy and Astrophysics, 1900–1975* (1979), provides a collection of seminal papers in the field, including much on stellar atmospheres, spectra, evolution and distribution, and variable stars. International technical reports of research in astronomical and astrophysical sciences can be found in the following periodicals: *The Astronomical Journal* (10/year) and *Astrophysical Journal* (3/month), both published by the American Astronomical Society; *Astronomy and*

Astrophysics (4/month); *Monthly Notices of the Royal Astronomical Society* (3/month); *Astrophysics* (quarterly), trans. from Russian; and *Chinese Astronomy and Astrophysics* (quarterly), trans. from Chinese. More popular articles are published in *Astronomy* (monthly); *The Journal of the American Association of Variable Star Observers* (semiannual); and *Sky and Telescope* (monthly).

UNDERSTANDING STAR CLUSTERS

Yu. N. Efremov, *Open Clusters, Associations, and Stellar Complexes* (1989), is a good, general-level introduction to star clusters and associations. Other overviews on broad aspects of the subject are Kenneth Janes (ed.), *The Formation and Evolution of Star Clusters* (1991); Keith N. Ashman and Stephen E. Zepf, *Globular Cluster Systems* (1998); and S.G. Djorgovski and G. Meylan (eds.), *Structure and Dynamics of Globular Clusters* (1993). Publications of symposia held by the International Astronomical Union are technical but informative; of particular interest are James E. Hesser (ed.), *Star Clusters* (1980); Jeremy Goodman and Piet Hut (eds.), *Dynamics of Star Clusters* (1985); and Piet Hut and Junichiro Makino (eds.), *Dynamical Evolution of Star Clusters: Confrontation of Theory and Observations* (1996). Arthur Cox (ed.), *Allen's Astrophysical Quantities*, 4th ed. (2000), contains useful tables and listings relating to star clusters.

NEBULAE

An excellent general reference work on all topics in astronomy, including all forms of nebulae, is Stephen P. Maran (ed.), *The Astronomy and Astrophysics Encyclopedia* (1992), with articles written for the technically trained person who is not familiar with astronomy. There are numerous articles written at a semitechnical level in the journals *Scientific American* (monthly); *Mercury* (bimonthly), published by the Astronomical Society of the Pacific; *Astronomy* (monthly); and *Sky and Telescope* (monthly). Readers with a thorough knowledge of physics may wish to consult Lyman Spitzer, Jr., *Physical Processes in the Interstellar Medium* (1978), very comprehensive and very terse; Donald E. Osterbrock and Gary J. Ferland, *Astrophysics of Gaseous Nebulae and Active Galactic Nuclei*, 2nd ed. (2006); and Sun Kwok, *Cosmic Butterflies: The Colorful Mysteries of Planetary Nebulae* (2001).

INDEX

A

absolute magnitude, explanation of, 18
Aldebaran A, 30, 31
Alpha Centauri, 18, 30, 38
Altair, 30
Ambartsumian, Victor A., 46
Andromeda galaxy, 70
Antares, 11, 31
Arcturus, 30, 31
astronomical unit, explanation of, 18

B

Bell, Jocelyn, 80
Bessel, Friedrich Wilhelm, 17
Betelgeuse, 19, 20, 31
binary/double star systems
    categories of, 30
    explanation of, 23
black dwarfs, 76
black holes, explanation of, 9, 74, 87–92
"blue straggler" problem, 51
Brahe, Tycho, 12
bright nebulae, 96–97, 100
brown dwarfs, 28–29, 41
Bruno, Giordano, 12

C

Canopus, 31
Capella A, 30
charge-coupled devices, 102
Coma Berenices, 43, 45, 63
Copernicus, Nicolaus, 11–12, 17
Crab Pulsar, 83

D

dark nebulae, 96, 97
Deneb, 18–19
diffuse ionized gas, 97, 98
dust of interstellar space, 109–113

E

eclipsing binaries, explanation of, 23
Einstein, Albert, 83, 87

G

Galileo Galilei, 12
glitches, 85
globular star clusters, 19, 43, 45, 47–54, 57, 62, 64, 66, 67, 69, 70, 71
gravitational contraction, 27, 32